Praise

'I found your book to be very readable and a great reference for anyone embarking on the redundancy process. A definite go-to! You give a good understanding of the process and great detail as to how to go about the steps towards redundancy... if one must.'
— **Wendy Martin Green**, Owner, Peter Green Furnishers

'I really enjoyed reading *Redundancy With Love* and I don't think I have read a book like this before – it really gets to the emotional side of redundancy, which is often ignored.'
— **Gurdip Singh**, Chief Executive Officer, Kallik

'It's clear you have been there and done it – I enjoyed reading it. I liked the anecdotes.'
— **Rupert Brice**, HR Change and Transformation Project Manager

'I think it will be a fabulous "bible" that people refer to when they are looking at this thorny subject matter and one which people can dip in and out of.'
— **Alex Hughes**, Director and Founder, Auxilium Business Consulting Ltd

'I enjoyed the honesty and the stories brought it to life. You have done a great job of capturing the elements around redundancy. Easy to read.'
— **Robin Farrar-Hockley**, Human Resources Consultant

JILL ABURROW

Redundancy with Love

Getting it right for your people and your business

Rᵉthink

First published in Great Britain in 2022
by Rethink Press (www.rethinkpress.com)

© Copyright Jill Aburrow

This book is dedicated to anyone who has ever faced redundancy, and to those who had to give them the message.

Contents

Foreword

If you have ever faced redundancy, you will know what an emotional rollercoaster it can be. If you have ever had the unpleasant task of telling someone in your team that they are going to be made redundant, you will have experienced that fear, concern and distaste for the task ahead. No matter how senior you are in an organisation, or how many times you have faced this task, it is always unpleasant.

As a senior manager in various global organisations, I have always disliked dealing with redundancies and the disruption they cause to even the best-regulated teams. The legal framework within the UK is such that there are regulations that have to be met. I have always had that niggling fear that an employment tribunal claim may follow a redundancy wave however well-managed the process might be. I have really relied on help from human resource professionals who can make the whole process feel less daunting.

Jill once supported me through a redundancy process within a large, global organisation. Her support was invaluable and she remained calm and focused through some trying conversations. At one point in that particular process, we found ourselves at an employment tribunal and I was very glad of Jill's support.

Jill's book is easy to read, logical and written in a way that anyone can understand. She doesn't confuse anyone with what I call 'technical babble', ie it's written in plain, understandable English. It is both informative and a good best practice to follow, making it easy for managers who need to go through this process. I liked the emphasis on the emotional sides of the process, both for the manager and for the employee – this is a tough activity and often people use the process to hide the emotional impact of what is happening. This book highlights the emotional sides well.

This stuff is not normally written down in one place; this book does that really well. As a manager you have many resources to go to but not one single source; this book provides a single source, joining up the dots.

One point that resonates with me is the need for managers to look after their own health and mental well-being when managing redundancies. Jill's point about having a safe place and/or person that enables you to let off steam and deal with your own emotions as a manager is key. Often, it's thought that managers who have to make someone redundant don't have any emotions and can just get on with their day: it is hard emotionally to do this whether you have done it once or one hundred times.

The chapter about consulting with the individual and giving the message is full of useful guidance. Knowing what to say is always hard. There is an important point in the chapter about trying to avoid too much small talk to put the person at ease. They will see through that and appreciate a more direct approach, as long as it is non-judgemental and clear and they can relate it to their own view of things.

Another part of the book that resonated with me was the chapter about the reactions of the employees whose roles are not being made redundant. Once a manager has made redundancies, I feel they are never again seen in the same light by remaining staff even if they followed the correct process, there was a genuine reason for the redundancies and everything has been handled fairly and with integrity. I think, as managers, we lose a certain bond and trust with staff once we deliver a redundancy activity, whether in a big or a small company, we are never seen in the same way. We have done the 'dirty' and redundancy is still a 'dirty' in many minds. Help to avoid these pitfalls is invaluable.

Whatever the size of your company or team, and however many times you have managed redundancies, there is plenty of information in this book to help ease your journey next time and to make it less stressful for everyone concerned – you, the people facing redundancy and those left behind afterwards.

Gurdip Singh
Chief Executive Officer, Kallik Ltd

Introduction

Redundancy is horrible. It is horrible for everyone, whether you're the person delivering the bad news, or the person facing the loss of their job.

For big employers, redundancy is a fairly regular part of working life – although managers within those businesses usually find it incredibly challenging. If you own a small business with fewer employees or you are a new manager within a larger organisation, it may not be something you have ever contemplated doing before. This may leave you feeling unprepared when the situation calls for it and, frankly, more than a little scared at the prospect. If you have spent time and effort building up trust and rapport with your work-force or team then having to make people redundant can feel like the ultimate betrayal.

Over the years, I have seen business owners and managers who are uncomfortable with the idea of redundancy. For many employers, the rules and legalities seem complex and the fear of getting it wrong can cause anxiety. There's plenty of information available on the internet about what to do, when to do it and how to comply with the law but, if you have never had to make someone redundant before and don't have the benefit of a trained in-house Human Resources (HR) team, it can be a scary process and one which seems fraught with danger.

When any group of people starts to talk about redundancy, there will be horror stories about how badly someone has been treated, what their employer did or did not do and how it made the redundant individual feel. If they are left feeling negative about the process and experience, they will blame their employer's poor communication and handling of the situation, and the employer's reputation will be impacted – whether or not that is a fair reflection of what happened. You will be faced with legal costs and the morale of your remaining employees is likely to be at a low ebb.

As a business owner or manager, you rightly value the hard-won reputation of your business with employees and customers alike. If disgruntled employees or ex-employees are spreading bad news about you in the pub or on social media, it won't take long for that to ripple out and become a big wave. Before you know it, your customers may start looking elsewhere and your business may be on a downward path. Your reputation as an employer and social media presence are damaged and it becomes an uphill struggle to recruit and retain good people.

I've written this book based on my experience as a HR manager to guide you through managing each stage of the redundancy cycle with love and without fear so that all parties can walk away from this most difficult of employment processes with full confidence that it could not have been done any better.

I have supported countless redundancy consultations over the years and I can confidently say that each one is different. I have seen every reaction imaginable, from an employee cheering and throwing his arms around his manager to threats of physical violence – denial, fear, tears and every emotion in between.

Like so many others, I have been on the other end of the process as well. I took voluntary redundancy from a previous employer and found it an interesting and challenging learning experience. Even in a voluntary situation, the way that an individual feels is largely dependent on how well the redundancy is handled.

There are many different reasons why employers need to consider making employees redundant and each comes with its own stresses. They are usually to do with financial difficulties or the loss of a particular customer or piece of work. The trauma of giving the message to your employees can make redundancy one of the most difficult challenges that a business can face. Redundancy is not a cheap option. If it is mishandled, the consequences can be far worse. If your employees can claim unfair dismissal or unfair selection for redundancy at an employment tribunal, the legal consequences can cost a lot of time and money – not to mention the effect on your reputation.

Every employer and manager I have worked with has wanted a step-by-step process to manage redundancy. That is fairly simple to provide – there are countless examples on the internet, including that of the Advisory, Conciliation and Arbitration Service (Acas).[1] I usually find that managers don't simply want to know what to do but *how* to do it. Why? They're afraid of getting it wrong. We all know the difficulty of consoling a bereaved friend – we're not sure what to say to help them cope – and it is the same for employers and managers faced with telling a valued employee that they no longer have a job. How can you tell them; what can you say to help them; what will be their reaction?

Businesses are also anxious about the legal implications of making redundancies: most are wary of unintentionally breaching the law. Disaffected employees who feel hurt and worried about the future often threaten that they're going to take their employer to an employment tribunal. No matter how confident an employer feels about its case for redundancy, employment tribunals can make unexpected judgements. It can be difficult to predict if something you thought was reasonable will turn out to be unlawful. Like every other HR practitioner and employment lawyer in the land, I cannot promise that you will be able to avoid this scenario entirely but, by following the steps and guidance in this book and treating people fairly and with compassion, the legalities are likely to fall into place naturally.

What about the people left behind in the business – the ones who have to pick up and carry on, often taking on tasks that their redundant colleagues used to do? The 'survivors' are often the forgotten factor in the redundancy process – yet, in many ways, they are more important to your business than those who have left. The survivors are the people who will carry your business forward and help it to bounce back, thrive and grow while you and your managers can take pride in how you handled a difficult situation.

To help you manage all of this, I am going to take you step by step through the redundancy cycle from when you first contemplate that you might need to make someone redundant, to selecting who is to go and consulting with them about it, to giving notice and paying their redundancy payment, right up to when they leave your employment and you look at rebuilding your business with your survivors.

The redundancy cycle

You will be looking at everything through a lens of love, compassion, kindness and 'doing the right thing'. This will lead you to the right answers for your business. It is not about paying lip service to the law and the Acas guidelines. It is about getting involved in every step and making it work for you, your employees, your customers, your business and your reputation. It is about helping your redundant employees move on to bigger and better things (and maybe even one day coming back to help you build your business). It is about helping your business to thrive and grow.

Yes, redundancy is horrible but it can also be a positive experience that reshapes your team or your business and propels your employees to even greater heights.

PART ONE
FIRST THOUGHTS

If your business is in temporary difficulty, you need to raise money quickly or you have a difficult person with whom you want to part company, it is easy to think that redundancy is the answer.[2] You need to carefully consider all options before you decide that redundancy is the way forward for your business. When contemplating redundancy, the first thing to do is look at all the possible alternatives and ways to avoid redundancies.

A well-managed redundancy process is a cycle of progressive stages. The process moves naturally from one step to the next step and the whole cycle revolves around a central tenet of collective consultation, which is a part of each stage. As we progress through this book (and the stages of the redundancy process), we will follow this cycle and refer back to the cycle diagram to confirm which step we are discussing.

The first part of the book starts with the 'review' stage of the process, which you might have assumed would come at the end of the cycle. It does – but it is also at the beginning. As you will see, it is a true cycle that starts and ends in the same place. We start with reviewing the need for redundancies and whether or not redundancy is the right solution for your business.

1

Review: Is Redundancy The Right Answer?

Redundancy is, sadly, a business norm these days. Many people have faced redundancy at least once in their working lives and they can find it damaging. It is often damaging for their employer as well.

There are many reasons why a business might need to consider redundancy as an option. In some cases, there is simply no choice – for example, if a business goes into administration because it is no longer viable. There may be an enforced hiatus in trading – for example, think of the effect that the coronavirus pandemic had on the travel and hospitality industries. More often, redundancy is a way of cutting costs or restructuring a team to maximise efficiency.

I would counsel any business to consider carefully before taking the difficult and drastic decision to make staff redundant. It is a risky option that can open your business to unwelcome conjecture and criticism. Making staff redundant is never a short-term solution to financial difficulties. Redundancy is an expensive business and it rarely brings the savings that are envisaged. The redundancy payments themselves can seem enormous, particularly if your employment contracts offer an enhanced redundancy package. On top of that, you also have to pay notice periods or pay in lieu of notice.

There are other financial drains, which may not be immediately obvious, such as the management time needed to plan, prepare and carry out a redundancy programme. If you are looking to save money, you may need to invest time in doing careful calculations. Remember that redundancy is an immediate outlay that is not spread over time.

Redundancy also means letting go of employees in whom you have invested and who might be hard to replace in future. It usually has a negative and unsettling impact on the staff who remain, which will inevitably lead to a drop in productivity. It is bad publicity and can lead to legal challenges unless handled carefully.

If your business has an uplift in the near future and you need more people, you may not be able to recruit again straight away. Even if you can, the people who were made redundant may no longer be available or willing to return. You will have to find the resources – money and time – to recruit again as well as deal with training up new staff. Accordingly, the first place to start when you are planning redundancy is to ask yourself if it is the right way forward for your business. This first chapter is about considering whether or not redundancy is the only or best option available to you.

What is the definition of redundancy?

Section 139 of the Employment Rights Act 1996 states that:

'an employee shall be taken to be dismissed by reason of redundancy if the dismissal is wholly or mainly attributable to—

(a) the fact that his employer has ceased or intends to cease—

(i) to carry on the business for the purposes of which the employee was employed by him, or

(ii) to carry on that business in the place where the employee was so employed, or

(b) the fact that the requirements of that business—

(i) for employees to carry out work of a particular kind, or

(ii) for employees to carry out work of a particular kind in the place where the employee was employed by the employer,

have ceased or diminished or are expected to cease or diminish.'[3]

In practice, the only valid reasons for redundancy are that the work your employees (or some of them) were employed to do has stopped, or that the need for that type of work has stopped or decreased or you are expecting it to stop or decrease. Anything else needs to be managed through another process. Dismissal is still possible in other circumstances – but not through redundancy.

What are you hoping to achieve?

The starting point in deciding whether or not redundancy is the best option is to look at what you are trying to achieve. There may no longer be the need for, or a decrease in the work of, some or all of your employees due to the loss of a large customer, new competition or an external factor (like a global pandemic). A seemingly quick way to cut your losses may be to reduce your employment overheads. Job cuts might save on salaries, benefits and employment costs like tax and national insurance contributions.

You could save on training, sick pay and holiday pay. This can seem attractive, but is it the saving it appears to be?

It is tempting to look at the obvious reductions in the costs of employing people, but there are other potential costs that you might incur afterwards – lower productivity, poor employee morale, lower levels of employee engagement and increased sickness. Although less visible and not as easily quantifiable, these can be damaging, especially when you are trying to rebuild your business. We explore the financial implications in more detail later on in the book.

If you are considering trying to use redundancy as a way to manage someone out of your business, ask yourself if this is a fair, right and lawful thing to do. (Clue: it isn't.) Maybe you have an employee who does not fit in with the rest of the team, is causing a bad atmosphere, is not performing well or takes a huge amount of time off sick. You may even have a disruptive employee or dislike someone's attitude. Some employers think that redundancy is a painless and kind way to dismiss someone 'difficult'. Letting them leave with a redundancy payment and the label of 'redundancy' feels more comfortable than dismissing them for misconduct or poor performance – but is redundancy the kindest and most effective way to manage this situation? The individual will go on to another employer, neither knowing that there was any problem. If the employee has not been given the chance to improve or try harder and is unaware of their shortcomings, how can they put things right? A new employer may hire the person in the firm belief that there were no problems, other than your need (as the previous employer) to restructure the work, and then find they are in for a world of trouble. It might work out well but there is a big risk that it won't.

Is it even lawful to manage a difficult employee in this way? The short answer is that it is not. This is not what redundancy is for (see the definition above) and there are strict legal constraints. If the employee decided to claim at employment tribunal that you had not put them through a fair selection process or you had mishandled the redundancy, the tribunal would likely agree with them. Losing at a tribunal will not do your reputation as an employer any favours. It can have a detrimental effect on the business – making recruitment difficult or it being harder to retain staff. If colleagues see that a difficult employee 'got away with it', even getting a nice redundancy payment, they are not going to trust you or want to remain with you for long. It has been known for employees who witness this situation to try to manipulate the process to get redundancy pay for themselves. False redundancy of this kind is not the cheapest option and it will not be the fairest solution.

Whatever your motivation for considering redundancy, there are likely to be options. Even if your business is closing – temporarily or permanently

– there may be other things you can consider before taking the huge step of declaring jobs redundant and forcing your employees to seek other employment.

Future goals and plans for the business

The starting point is to map out the future of your business. Once you know the goals and plans you want to achieve, say, in the next five years, you can think about what skills and experience your workforce will need to enable the business to achieve those goals. This is workforce planning and it is a crucial tool for businesses, large and small.

Your business planning and forecasting will inform your workforce plan. It is wise to build in as much flexibility as possible – multiskilling, job flex and flexible terms and conditions of employment, work times and locations. This can help you plan your vacancies and recruitment needs as well as guard against potential redundancies.

It is important that you understand your contract/order pipeline and know which contracts are due to expire in the next few years and when. Consider what work you are expecting to come in and the impact this might have on your workforce so that you can include this in the workforce plan.

You should also consider what happens if you lose a contract to a competitor. In this circumstance, the people in your company who were doing that work will likely transfer employment to the competitor to continue doing so. This process is known as the Transfer of Undertakings (Protection of Employment) or TUPE. The TUPE regulations protect employees' rights when they transfer to a new employer.[4] If TUPE applies to a contract you lose to a competitor, it will potentially save jobs and prevent redundancies.

Your workforce plan should reveal the future skills you need. You may have those skills in your business already which is a great start when you need to consider whether or not redundancies are desirable or even necessary. What can your current employees already provide? They may have skills and experience that are not currently being used but are crucial to your vision for your business.

This might be the time to do a skills audit. You will be able to assess what gaps there are and where there might be a glut of specific skills. This data will help to inform your decision about whether or not redundancy is necessary and will come in useful if the redundancy goes ahead and you need to start selecting which employees to keep. An employee might not like the fact that their job is at risk of redundancy but the pill might be a little easier to swallow if they can see that the decision has been based fairly and squarely on a need for skills and experience that they cannot provide.

The true costs – is it worth it?

If you are facing the difficult decision to make staff redundant, take the time to do careful calculations. It is not always the best way to cut costs and keep your business alive. A cost-versus-benefit analysis of a redundancy programme might prove informative.

The immediate financial benefits for any employer are obvious. Salaries no longer have to be paid to those people. You don't have the employment costs such as tax and national insurance. You save on their pension contributions. There might also be a saving in management costs. With fewer people to manage, there could be the option to reduce your management team. Managers may need to spend less time managing the people who are left.

There are also obvious costs to making someone redundant. If they have over two years' service, they are entitled to a statutory redundancy payment, which can be up to thirty weeks' pay depending on their age and length of service.[5] They may be entitled to an enhanced redundancy payment if there is such a clause in their contract of employment. You also have to continue to pay their salary while the consultation is ongoing (which may be weeks or months) and during their notice period. You might make a payment to them in lieu of notice if you want them to leave sooner or pay for them to be on garden leave if their contracts of employment allow for these.[6] If any unused holiday entitlement is accrued, you have to give them that time off before they leave (on full pay) or pay them in lieu.[7] You must also allow them reasonable time off to seek alternative employment on full pay.[8]

ASSESS THE LONG-TERM COSTS

My husband and I bought a beaten-up old Mercedes a few years ago. We knew she needed some work, but we thought she would be an investment as her value would go up once the work was done.

Five years on, we now have a beautiful classic but she still needs work (I'm not sure it will ever finish). She is worth a great deal more than when we first bought her, but we are still running at a loss – she has cost far more than we thought. Every time we fixed one issue, it revealed something far more serious.

Even though a decision looks financially sound, it can pay to look into it in more depth before you decide to go ahead. This is true in business too and is definitely the case with redundancy. On the face of it, redundancy is a way to save money fast. It immediately cuts salaries, employment costs, benefits and pensions, but it can often end up costing more than it saves.

Other expenses may not be immediately obvious. This may be where you find that the true price of redundancy starts to mount up. These include your time and your managers' time to plan, prepare and carry out a redundancy programme; the time doing any scoring needed for selection; the time needed for consultation and to plan the remaining workload. The managers doing this work are likely to be among the highest paid. They will not be productive on other things while they are involved in a redundancy process. In addition, there is your payroll staff's time to work out all of the redundancy and other payment calculations and make the relevant payments, plus your HR team and/or managers' time writing and providing references. Again, while they are doing this, they are not working on more productive things for your business.

If you recognise trade unions (TUs), your TU representatives will be occupied with the process during this time. If you don't recognise trade unions and you are planning more than twenty redundancies, you will have to arrange a secret ballot to elect employee representatives to enable collective consultation.[9] However many redundancies you are planning, TU representatives or other colleagues might be asked to accompany individuals in any consultation meetings.[10] All of that costs their time and productivity.

There are many other small things that form part of the process, including time to hold meetings, answer questions and consider suggestions. Even in a well-managed redundancy process, the biggest (and most incalculable) hidden cost is the lost productivity of the workforce. Productivity levels take time to build up again to pre-redundancy levels.

If you want people to leave the workplace before their notice period ends or if the reason for the redundancy is a lack of work, you may need to pay them to go on garden leave. On the other hand, if a customer contract is coming to an end, you may need to keep redundant employees for a set period to finish the remaining work to complete that contract. There is a fine balance, but you may need to pay a retention bonus or other incentive payment to ensure a redundant employee remains motivated and engaged while they complete any outstanding work.

Some companies provide outplacement services for their redundant employees to help them find alternative work or train for a career change, which have a cost attached. You may want to provide counselling services to help your employees and their families come to terms with their redundancy or financial advice to help them manage their redundancy pay, pensions, etc. Counselling may not be enough to prevent sickness absence if individuals have anxiety, depression or other stress-related illnesses due to impending redundancy. Your sick pay bill may go up during this time, not just for those facing redundancy but also for their colleagues who remain in the workplace after they leave.

On the subject of those who stay, training in new skills for people who have had to move into different jobs or pick up unfamiliar work may be necessary. Before considering making permanent employees redundant, you could also need to end any third-party contractors or temporary agency staff and pay fees to employment agencies.

Do factor in potential costs associated with legal challenges and having to pay lawyers or barristers' fees to defend such challenges or for a settlement agreement to prevent a court case, not to mention staff time to work on such cases.

Some expenses will crop up later that must be included in the overall figures for redundancy, as they arise only as a result of the redundancy programme. They include payment for future advertising of vacancies and any recruitment if there is an upturn. You may end up trying to recruit the very skills you let go and paying to train people up into these roles having lost the investment in your redundant employees. Depending on how well your redundancy programme was handled, your company's reputation may suffer leaving you finding it harder to recruit in the future. You may even face resignations as people search for potentially more stable employment.

One final potential cost is in your client base. If the reputation of your business suffers due to the redundancy, you may lose clients or find it hard to attract new business.

Cost checklist – tangible and intangible costs

Tangible costs	£	Intangible costs	£
Statutory redundancy payments		Managers' time (planning, training, dealing with questions, loss of productivity)	
Enhanced redundancy payments		TUs, representatives, colleagues, individuals facing redundancy – time lost in consultations	
Outplacement costs		Staff time doing financial calculations	
Counselling (individuals facing redundancy; managers; survivors)		Staff time writing references	
Financial counselling for redundant staff		Lost productivity (whole workforce)	
Redundancy enhancements to encourage acceptance of settlement agreements		Sickness/sick pay (likely to increase during redundancy programme)	
Garden leave		Legal costs if any challenge; staff/ legal advisor time in producing settlement agreements	
Pay in lieu of notice		Time spent dealing with appeals	

Tangible costs	£	Intangible costs	£
Unused annual leave		Training new skills for survivors	
Notice pay		Reputation	
Agency fees (if dismissing agency staff) – see agreement with agency		Future recruitment for skills lost in redundancy programme	

Summary

Redundancy might seem the ideal solution to a business issue but it is expensive and hugely time-consuming. It often does not bring the required cost reductions. I do suggest that you carefully weigh up all of the implications of redundancy and how long it will take your business to recover from such a move. The business case for your redundancies needs to be carefully constructed with facts and figures that will be considered thoroughly during collective consultation.

Not only does it mean letting go of employees in whom you have invested and who might be hard to replace in future, but it usually negatively impacts those who remain in your employment. As the old saying goes 'trust takes years to build and seconds to destroy' – that applies to employees and customers. It creates bad publicity for your business and can lead to legal challenges unless handled carefully. You can expect the business to be challenged internally – and potentially externally – as part of any legal dispute. Redundancy is not an easy process and can be immensely damaging.

Redundancy is not the only answer. It may seem the simplest and cheapest way forward but look at alternatives before committing to redundancies. We consider the possible alternatives in the next chapter.

2

Review: Alternatives To Redundancy

As we established in Chapter 1, redundancy is not always the best answer. Even if you are planning a redundancy programme, it is important that you first think about the alternatives to making someone redundant. You may have already considered – and possibly rejected – other options but it is worth revisiting and giving serious thought to whether or not any of the alternatives could work. If you can save just one job, that is a success.

In this chapter, we look at possible alternatives to redundancy and consider the advantages and disadvantages. This will help you to decide whether you have explored all of the options before you commit to a redundancy process.

What alternatives are possible?

Firstly, you will need a thorough understanding of your business financials to assess whether redundancy is the only option or if other cost reductions could be made instead to mitigate the need for redundancy.

Consider the following:

- Are there other roles within the business that those who would face redundancy could fill? You may already have approved vacancies, or it may be that managers were at the stage of considering whether they needed to recruit an extra person. This can also include retraining staff to do different roles.

- Can you implement a recruitment freeze? It seems perverse to be recruiting while you are letting staff go elsewhere. Review current and forthcoming vacancies and pare them down to the bare minimum (zero, if possible – at least temporarily).

- How can you maximise staff flexibility as an alternative to recruiting staff who would need to be made redundant at a later date?

- Can any of the work be adapted or dropped (temporarily or permanently)?

- Can you recycle, reuse or repair furnishings, equipment or tools instead of renewing them to save costs?

- Can you make reductions in costs such as non-essential travel, company vehicles, subsidised cafeteria, etc?

- Are there any grants or incentives available from the government or elsewhere that could help you through a sticky financial period?

- Can you limit the number of contractors and agency staff you are using? Are they doing work that could be carried out by an employee instead?

- Could you offer your employees an option similar to the government's furlough scheme during the global pandemic? For example, you could offer to pay them a percentage of their salary (the government's scheme was 80%) for a period during which they don't do any work. This might seem costly – to pay people not to work – but it reduces your costs and keeps them on your payroll. It might be viable for a short-term period. Beware though, there are legalities and it has to have been agreed upon with employees beforehand.[11]

- Other alternatives might include offering sabbaticals, reduced hours / working days or salary reductions, and looking at secondment or redeployment opportunities. For a small business, this could even be done in conjunction with your local competitors – collaboration on staffing issues can help you both.[12]

- Communicate and consult with your employees as they might have ideas. They have a vested interest in helping you to save their jobs.

This list is not exhaustive. Get creative – there may be other things you can do to avoid some or all of your redundancies.

WOULD YOU TAKE A SALARY CUT TO SAVE JOBS?

I did a poll on LinkedIn asking whether people would take a salary cut to prevent redundancies in their workplace. The respondents came from a variety of working backgrounds – small business owners, managers in larger businesses and leaders in large or multinational organisations. The possible answers ranged from 'no, I need every penny' to 'yes, if it saved some jobs'. There were other qualified 'yes' answer options.

I understand why someone might answer 'no' in these difficult times, and I expected more people to do so, but the overwhelming majority (90%) gave a qualified 'yes' answer. To me, this illustrates that considering some kind of salary cut – temporary or not – is a valid and useful way for businesses to avoid redundancies. Proper care is necessary to make it work and ensure it is legal. You need to take HR or legal advice if it is something you would like to consider for your business.

I have seen it suggested that if high salaries in the UK were capped at between £100,000 and £300,000, it could save up to a million jobs.[13] This covers a small percentage of the highest paid – an income of even £100,000 is likely to put you in the top 4–5% of earners – but it made me think about smaller companies with more modest wage bills. A company's wage bill is likely to be a large – if not the largest – portion of their expenditure, which is why redundancy is often seen as a good way to cut costs. When I advise business leaders and managers about ways to avoid redundancy, capping their highest salaries is among the alternatives I suggest they should consider.

What have you rejected and why?

You may have already considered some of the suggestions in the list of possible alternatives and rejected them as impractical for some reason, but it is worth looking again in depth before you rule them out. Keep an open mind when you are looking at potential alternatives to redundancy. The most important thing is to consult with your employees. Employees often see things in a completely different light from managers and company owners. No matter how well you know your staff, you might find that they surprise you.

If you are a small employer, you may think that none of these alternatives is possible for a business of your size. Have you thought about joining forces with your competitors or other small businesses in your local area? If other businesses are facing similar struggles, you might be able to pool resources and even share employees. It can be helpful to think laterally about a problem. There may be nothing you can do in practical terms but if you can show that you have considered every possible angle, your employees will accept the inevitable more easily and your reputation as an employer will remain intact.

GENUINE CONSULTATION

In my early years in HR, I worked at a company that needed to make cost reductions, so they announced a redundancy process. At one of the first collective consultation meetings with TU and other employee representatives, an employee suggested that the company should stop providing free tea and coffee for staff. None of the managers had considered this option. There were several reasons why it might have been rejected – perhaps they thought it wouldn't save much money, employees would resist having a benefit taken away or the business would be seen in a negative light.

As it had been suggested in formal consultation, the management team took the idea away and looked into it. They discovered that if the company ceased providing tea, coffee, milk and biscuits for the entire workforce, the cost saving over a year was the equivalent of the salary of one employee. It would prevent one of the redundancies.

When the suggestion was put to the employees, they overwhelmingly accepted it as everyone was keen to save a job. The managers had been worried about negative feedback from employees for stopping a benefit, but they achieved positive results by being open to employee suggestions and carrying out a genuine consultation.

The experience taught me not to make assumptions about what employees will and will not accept in terms of alternatives. It also showed the benefit of open and honest consultation.

Summary

There are numerous alternatives to redundancy. While some might not seem viable for your business, it is always worth giving all careful consideration. If nothing else, it is important to be able to show that you have considered every option and given serious thought to whether the redundancy programme should go ahead. Consulting with your staff can bring unexpected suggestions and help them to come to terms with the need to look at cutting staff numbers.

PART TWO
PLANNING

Once you have decided that redundancy is the best way forward, the next step is to decide how many jobs should be made redundant and which people to select. This is the time to start the first and, arguably, the most important stage in a redundancy process: planning.

The foundation for any redundancy programme is your redundancy policy. If you don't have one, it is a good idea to produce one. Your policy tells your employees and their representatives what to expect and the process you will follow. If you have a policy that follows Acas guidelines and you stick to that policy, you won't go far wrong.[14]

It is important to decide on things like how you will select people for redundancy, whether you will allow volunteers, how you will consult with your employees and what support you will offer. In particular, there are specific requirements if you are facing more than twenty redundancies.[15]

The second part of the planning process is to ensure that you and your managers have had training in redundancy processes: how to select people fairly, how to avoid unconscious bias, how to manage difficult conversations, how to give employees the difficult message and the legal pitfalls to avoid. If your managers are trained to deal with these situations, they will be better prepared for the difficult task of telling someone that they are likely to lose their job.

3

Plan: Your
Redundancy Plan

Although redundancy happens all the time in business, that does not mean it is familiar or easy for your managers or your employees. There are ways to improve this process for everyone involved. One way to make it easier is to have a plan that you can stick to and that will help you to cover all of the bases.

This book is called *Redundancy With Love*, but how can love possibly have anything to do with redundancy? Redundancy is uncomfortable and unpleasant for everyone, so where is the love in that? The key is the way you (and your managers) handle the process and the compassion, kindness, dignity and fairness you build into it. It is more than the legalities (although they are important); it is about how it leaves people feeling – that includes the business leaders and managers giving the message and those left behind after redundancy as well as those losing their jobs.

I have also heard of employers that announce the risk of redundancies, go through the whole consultation and selection process and confirm redundancies, only to do a U-turn at the last minute and cancel the redundancies. This is bad for everyone concerned. The employee facing redundancy has reached the point of accepting their fate and started to plan for and look forward to a different future. Suddenly they are expected to carry on as before in a job in which they have probably lost interest and no longer feel secure. With egg on their face, the employer has to explain the situation to the employee (and colleagues) and may have to try to buy back trust and loyalty through financial compensation. This situation can be avoided by sensible planning.

How to plan with compassion

My top tips for making sure that love, kindness and compassion are included in your planning are as follows:

- Ensure that you have explored all the alternatives and that redundancy is absolutely necessary.

- Make sure your process and procedures are fair, transparent, consistent and properly implemented.

- Create – and regularly update – a communications plan to ensure consistency.

- Make sure your method of selecting which employees to make redundant is fair, transparent and easily explained.

- Make sure you allocate enough time for consultation and that it answers all the employees' questions. Prepare properly and make sure there is plenty of time and no distractions. Make sure the individuals are accompanied if they want to be, they understand what you are telling them and they have the opportunity to ask questions. Thank them for their hard work and dedication, make them feel valued and make sure they know it is not their fault.

- Ensure they have the chance to apply for other roles you have available. Give them time off to look for alternative jobs.

- Don't give false hope about jobs or the possibility of re-employment at a later date.

- Make sure the employee is the focus of the consultation. A manager complaining about how hard or time-consuming it is or even relating a story about when they were made redundant in the past will not help the employee who is going through it now. It will increase their feeling of being worthless and valueless to the organisation.

- Provide any help you can (introductions to other employment opportunities, training, CV writing, references, financial advice, counselling) but don't promise things you cannot deliver.

- Make sure the redundancy payments are calculated properly and paid on time. Make sure the person facing redundancy is clear about the payment they will get and when it will be paid. Mistakes and delays in payments do not make someone feel valued.

- Look after yourself. Have a safe place where and/ or person with whom you can let off steam and deal with your own emotions.

- Make sure you support those who remain behind after redundancies. Explain everything to them in full and make sure they feel valued and secure.

Your redundancy policy and procedure

In the introduction to this section on planning, I recommended having a redundancy policy in place. A policy lays out what your intentions and approach will be in a redundancy situation and the procedures you will follow and expect others to follow. The redundancy policy will probably be in your company handbook and should be given out to employees when they start work and whenever the policy is updated.[16] It is a point of reference for your employees so they know what to expect. It can help you to defend your process at an employment tribunal and can also act as a reminder to cover all of the necessary steps. It will give your managers confidence. A policy that is based on the Acas guidelines on redundancy will be a marker in the ground that you, as an employer, are prepared to do things fairly and properly.[17]

If you are planning redundancies in your workplace, it is important to ensure you have a fair redundancy process in place. Your policy and plan will demonstrate this. Employees who have been with you for more than two years can claim unfair dismissal if there is not a fair redundancy process. It is also a kind and compassionate thing to do. A fair process ensures you have the right people in place to take your business forward and it is a way of capitalising on one of your most costly investments – your employees.

The basic requirements of a fair process are:[18]

- Consultation: anyone who *might* be at risk of redundancy must have the opportunity of at least one individual consultation meeting *before* any final decision is made.

- Employees must be informed how long the process will take, how people will be selected and how to appeal if they are selected for redundancy.

- If you have to select between more than one employee doing the same job, the selection criteria must be objective and transparent.

- If suitable alternative work exists, employees facing redundancy must be offered it (if they meet the basic requirements).

- If you are looking at more than twenty redundancies, there should be a collective consultation, which must start at least thirty days before any redundancy happens.

- If you are looking at more than 100 redundancies, the collective consultation must start at least forty-five days before any redundancy happens.

These six requirements are the bare minimum required legally. My advice in your handling of these processes is to make sure that they are as kind, fair and compassionate as possible for everyone concerned – managers, redundant employees and remaining employees.

Here are some questions you need to think about carefully and include in your plan. They are not meant to give quick and easy answers but to act as pointers.

- How will you explain the business case for the redundancy? How much information will you provide about finances and plans?

- How will you control communications to stop the rumour mill from taking over?

- How will your communications plan take into account different stakeholder groups (including external bodies) and ensure consistent messaging?

- What support are you giving those made redundant to find other work?

- How meaningful is your consultation? Have you been open to suggestions about how redundancy can be avoided?

- How fair is your selection process?

- Have you kept the door open for a future employment relationship or have you burnt your bridges?

- What support are you offering those who have 'survived' redundancy and remain employed by you?

- What steps are you putting in place to avoid future redundancy?

- Are you using the redundancy process to 'get rid of deadwood'? (Clue: if so, this raises big question marks about your management style.) As described previously, redundancy is not the right way to achieve this type of dismissal.

- How fair and kind is your whole redundancy process?

- If you, your partner or your children were to be made redundant by your company, would you feel you or they have been treated fairly and kindly?

'Unfair reasons for redundancy'

You and your managers will need an overview of the legalities behind redundancy – or include some training on this in your redundancy plan. Most importantly, all involved in the process need to be aware that UK law considers certain situations to be 'automatically unfair reasons for redundancy'.[19] This means that if an employment tribunal finds you have breached the relevant rules, it is an unfair dismissal whatever your defence or reasons might be.

The following are the automatically unfair circumstances for redundancy:

1. All workers, regardless of how long they have worked for you, have a right not to be discriminated against. Under the Equality Act 2010, workers are protected from being discriminated against on grounds of race, disability, sex, religion or belief, pregnancy and maternity, being married, sexual orientation, transgender status or age.[20]

2. Employees who have worked for you for more than two years can claim unfair dismissal if there has not been a fair redundancy process.[21]

3. It is unlawful to dismiss an employee for upholding one of their workplace rights: for example, asking for holiday, making a complaint about health and safety, joining a trade union

or whistleblowing about the employer doing something unlawful.[22] Employees must be able to discuss or enforce their rights without fear of reprisals.

How can you avoid these pitfalls? A fair redundancy process will go a long way to mitigating the risk of a legal challenge. It is unrealistic to think you will never see an employment claim – there will always be employees who feel they have been treated unfairly and raise a claim (some even do it to waste time and money as an act of 'revenge') – but the risks are much lower if you treat your employees kindly and fairly and genuinely do your best for them.

Any claim is far easier to defend if you can clearly show a fair process. You might be convinced your process was fair but if you can't demonstrate this with a clear paper trail of evidence such as documents that reinforce your business case, minutes of consultation meetings and objective scoring against selection criteria, you could nevertheless lose at a tribunal. Standard note-keeping formats, checklists, policies and procedures will help your management team deliver consistency.

What needs to be included in your redundancy plan?

The redundancy policy outlines the bare necessities and expectations of any redundancy process. When you are facing a redundancy situation, you also need to create a plan for that specific redundancy programme.

Your redundancy plan should be shared with trade unions and / or employee representatives so that it can be discussed and form the basis of the collective consultation that you must do if more than twenty people are to be made redundant (see Chapter 5).[23] Following collective consultation, it will need to be shared with all staff so that they know what is going to happen whether or not they are selected for redundancy.

A well-written plan, which has been consulted upon and shared with staff, can help you to follow a fair process. As well as the positive impact this can have on your staff, it will help to avoid the risk of any legal claims.

Your plan should include all of the alternatives you have considered before deciding on making redundancies. It is helpful if you can include why those alternatives have been rejected (or were not enough to prevent redundancy). The plan should also outline the number of redundancies you are considering and what areas of the business are affected. This may change slightly throughout the process, but the plan needs to give an idea of how many people are likely to face redundancy. This will be a time of anxiety for all of your employees, which can be lessened if they have an idea of the number of redundancies that are planned and which jobs need to go.

It is important to include a clear communications plan and ensure that it covers all potential stakeholders and who should be given what information and when. The plan should detail how you will keep staff informed throughout the process and what support is available to them. This must include anyone who is currently off work on sick leave, maternity leave or sabbatical, etc.

You must decide whether your plan will allow people to volunteer for redundancy and, if so, how you will decide whether or not they can be accommodated. Voluntary redundancy is a double-edged sword. On the one hand, it feels like an easy win – someone wants to go, which saves a compulsory redundancy. On the other hand, you risk losing your best employees (those who will find it easier to get alternative work) and the people you end up keeping may not have the right skills. I discuss this more in Chapter 6 about selection.

Your plan should also include details of how any selection will be made (ie the selection criteria you intend to use). You may need to ensure you have considered the specific impact on disabled or pregnant employees, those on maternity or paternity leave, Black, Asian and minority ethnic (BAME) employees and those who have any other protected characteristics.[24] We talk further about selection and consultation later in the book.

A good plan should also include details of redundancy payment calculations (whether they are statutory or contractual) and the same for notice periods.

Finally, the plan should cover how an employee can appeal if they think their selection or the process was unfair. You can see from this that planning for redundancies is not quick or easy and requires serious effort and consideration to make sure that the balance is right for your business. The object is to end up with a more streamlined workforce that is well equipped to take you into the future. That takes careful planning.

Redundancy timeline planning

It is helpful if you can specify timeframes for the process, including for collective and individual consultation and for managers to do the selection process (if there is one). It is critical to allow plenty of time to complete each stage. A rushed process in which the stakeholders have to make decisions under too much time pressure is likely to mean that opportunities to save jobs are missed. It can also open the organisation up to a claim of unfairness. You might find the following timeline tool useful to complete as part of your planning.

Redundancy timeline planning sheet

Key step in the process	Estimated timeline
Pre-redundancy planning and business case	
Initial communications	
Elect representatives	
Brief/train managers	
Brief/train representatives	
Prepare payment calculations	
Prepare employee support/ outplacement	
Collective consultation	Ensure you meet statutory period
Manage communications and FAQ process	
Finalise redundancy pool(s)	
Apply selection criteria to those in pools	
Individual consultation	
Prepare settlement agreements, if necessary	
Give notice or arrange payment in lieu of notice/ garden leave	
Manage any appeals	
Manage payments to those leaving	
Manage full record keeping of rationale and decisions	Ongoing

Vacancies and contractors or temporary staff

In my experience, something that can upset people placed at risk of redundancy is seeing that the company is still recruiting, filling vacancies and employing contractors or temporary staff. They feel that if the company needs to save money and declare redundancies, how can it continue to recruit new people and employ expensive contractors? Your planning should include how you will manage vacant positions and recruitment during the redundancy process.

Your first instinct is probably to freeze all recruitment. This might be the most pragmatic and popular stance, however, you may have vacancies for roles that are critical to the future success of your business but lack the relevant skills within the company already or any potential internal candidates for the roles. You could look at postponing the recruitment until the redundancies have taken place.

It may be unavoidable to keep approving job offers and recruitment plans, even in the light of forthcoming redundancies. If so, you must be able to demonstrate a clear business case for continued recruitment and it must be transparent and easily explained to potentially redundant employees. It is certainly not fair or acceptable to continue to recruit for skills that you have already within the potentially redundant population. Bear in mind that you may be unaware of other skills they have but do not currently use – something to be clarified during the consultation.

If you use contractors and temporary staff, you need to decide how the proposed redundancy will affect them. If they are in a different area of the business than the one affected by redundancy, you may not need to change anything. Sometimes, there is a sound economic business reason to keep your contractors or recruit new people, but you need to be able to explain that to those who are at risk of losing their jobs in such a way that they can understand the reasoning.

Another difficult area to consider is any staff on fixed-term contracts with an agreed and defined end date for the specific piece of work they were contracted to do. It seems simple and fair to the contractors to think that you will keep them on until the end of their contract. Again, though, it can be a source of anxiety for employees who are told they are at risk of redundancy. The human tendency is to compare ourselves to others and they may feel it reflects negatively on their abilities. In some respects, it may be better to give notice to all your fixed-term contractors that they will finish on a set date (before the redundancies). Again, this needs careful consideration and it will depend on the specific circumstances in your business at the time.

Much of this decision-making will depend on your future goals and plans and how the skills of your fixed-term contractors fit into those plans. If they are valuable future skills, you may want to use the fixed-term contractors to transfer those skills to some of your permanent (and potentially redundant) employees. If that is not an option, you may keep the fixed-term contractors but you should prepare a response to the trade unions, employee representatives and staff about why you need to keep them.

Apprentices, interns and work placements

Another group of people who need specific consideration when it comes to redundancy are any apprentices or interns in your business. If you have work placement students, there is not usually any cost involved and you are probably safe to keep using them as before. They will not cause contention with your employees who are at risk of redundancy.

Apprentices and interns are a different matter. In some ways, the easiest solution is to include them in the selection pools with others doing the same or similar work but you have to guard against scoring them lower because they have little experience or incomplete skills. You will also need to consider what will happen to their training plans if you let them go and ensure you consult with any third party who is involved. On the other hand, if you decide not to include apprentices and interns in your selection pools, consider carefully how this will be received by those who are in the pools.

It is key to weigh up the potential future benefit of apprentices and interns against the difficulty and cost involved in including them in the selection pool and the feelings of your employees who will be placed at risk. This is something that it may be wise to consult collectively about (see Chapter 5).

Plan the help you will offer your redundant employees

While you are at the stage of planning your redundancy programme, you might want to consider what help you can offer to redundant employees. The minimum you must do by law is to give them paid time off to help them job-hunt.[25] There are many other things that you can choose to do. Most employers are prepared to provide references to potential new employers, although these are often limited to basic details of when someone worked for you and what job they did. It is kinder and more helpful to your employees if you can provide more tailored references which highlight their strengths and skills for a new employer.

Large corporate companies often offer something called outplacement. Third-party outplacement providers work with redundant employees to help them decide what they want to do next, whether that is finding a new job, changing careers or doing training. Outplacement providers can also provide a personal career plan and help them with networking opportunities. They can give advice and guidance on self-employment or working on a contract basis. They can also help employees to understand the current job market and methods of job hunting. If someone has been in the job for a long time, they may not know how to go about searching for something new. An outplacement provider will help with creating CVs and teaching how to use LinkedIn or job sites. If someone is nearing retirement age, an outplacement provider can advise on retirement preparation. There is much support available and it will depend on how much you can afford to spend and the type of employees in your workforce.

You might consider providing confidential counselling to help individuals and/or their families come to terms with the reality of their situation and deal with the accompanying stress and anxiety. Another option is financial planning guidance, which can be useful to help people manage their finances while they seek alternative work and make their redundancy payment last as long as possible. They may need some guidance about finances in retirement. It might be possible to commute some or all of their redundancy payment into a pension. For this, you may need to bring in pension and retirement professionals or independent financial advisors.

Once you have decided what help and support you can provide, it should be included in your redundancy plan. When you consult with your employees about the potential redundancies, they may also have further suggestions of help that they need. You can then decide what you will offer consistently to all employees facing redundancy. We cover this topic in more detail in Chapter 8.

Summary

In this chapter, we have explored how to plan for your redundancy programme and what you need to include in that plan. We have discussed your redundancy policy and why you need one. We have considered what you must do depending on how many employees are facing redundancy. In terms of organising and consultation about that plan, the more support and help you can offer your employees the better.

The way a redundancy is handled and the help that is offered will mark you out as a great employer. Remember that disgruntled employees may be quick to post stories of their poor treatment on social media, particularly on sites such as Glassdoor which are widely used by potential recruits to evaluate their future employers. This can be incredibly damaging when it is time to recruit later.

It is always encouraging to hear stories from employees who felt their employers cared and handled their redundancy well. I often hear the horror stories. You want your company to be included in the positive ones.

4
Plan: Support For Managers

If you want your business to get redundancy right, your managers are the key to your success. They have to give the difficult message and provide support. Often, managers have not had to make redundancies before and they find it daunting. Like any other process, they need training and they also need support. Sometimes they are facing redundancy themselves while having to deal with making people in their teams redundant. This is a horrible situation to be in and a good employer can do a huge amount to help lessen the stress.

Training and supporting your managers is a big part of your redundancy planning. Your managers are ambassadors for your business in redundancy as in everything else they do. If you help them to do it well, your business and everyone concerned will benefit.

In this chapter, we are going to look at what training and support managers might need and the mindset they need to develop. We will also touch on the legalities that managers need to understand.

Giving the message

I have said it before – redundancy is hard on everyone involved and that includes the person who is giving the message. Whether it is the business owner, a manager or an HR professional, I have yet to meet anyone who finds redundancy easy or likes doing it. As leaders, we sometimes have to do things we don't enjoy. If you are a business leader and you employ other people, there may come a time when you have to give the redundancy message to someone.

As with all things, it can be easier with proper preparation and training in what to expect and how to handle things. Our redundancy plan needs to include a section about training for managers. They need to know why redundancies are being made and understand the details of the redundancy plan. You need to help them feel confident to talk to employees (those facing redundancy and others) about the redundancy process. They also need to know how to get answers to questions and how to raise suggestions and concerns they or the staff might have. It may be that they need training in running meetings (face-to-face and remotely), holding difficult conversations and dealing with different responses to the news.

If your managers have been involved from the start and kept informed about the process, they will be able to answer questions from employees. They will be able to bring their own ideas and suggestions to the process. They can offer ideas about avoiding or reducing the number of redundancies. They will be able to make redundancy dismissals and give the appropriate notice to those selected for redundancy. They will also be in a much better position to help the people who remain and the business to move forward after the redundancies.

I have supported some organisations that provided a pre-prepared script to guide managers on what to say to their team members facing redundancy. This can help ensure that the manager covers every aspect and reduce their nerves about what to say. The downside of this approach is sometimes managers merely read the script by rote. This takes any personal feelings out of the situation and can squash the compassion or care that the employee is likely to need. When the employee asks a question or makes a point, it can be difficult for the manager to cope as there is no script for how to answer those questions and points. A simple checklist can be better so that the manager can make sure they have covered all the necessary points. Both approaches have their merits.

Sometimes, managers want to 'make things easier' for the people in their team. This is only natural but some managers can make premature promises to their 'favourites' that they will not be affected. This can cause enormous problems later on if such promises cannot be kept. The manager's favourite may not be able to keep their job even if the manager tries to ensure the selection process works in their favour. This needs to be highlighted to managers when they are preparing for the redundancy process – they need to know the consequences of such promises.

Managers should be advised to make notes as they go. Notes of the consultation meeting can be helpful afterwards when both parties might find it difficult to remember what was covered. A well-written checklist or script (as above) can help with producing such notes. It is also critical to record any commitments that are made to those facing redundancy to ensure that they are followed up and the employee gets the support they are expecting.

Preparation is the key to making the process work smoothly. It is the reason for having a redundancy plan in the first place and it is also important on an individual basis for the managers who are giving the message.

PREPARATION IS KEY

We all make mistakes. They are learning points and building blocks for the future.

Some time ago, I worked with a company that needed to announce redundancies.

It was agreed that everyone should get the same information on the same day to ensure timely and consistent messaging. People who were out of the workplace would be visited at home and given the same information.

One line manager duly went out to visit an employee who was on annual leave. The employee answered the door with the words 'I do hope you haven't come to make me redundant on my birthday.' The manager, who had no idea it was the individual's birthday, was horrified because that was exactly the purpose of the visit.

It was an uncomfortable lesson – and is an example of business leaders and employees not seeing things in the same light. The company's intention was good – that the message was clear and given to all at the same time – but the employee saw it as an unkind act.

The lesson for me was to always check the small details so you can be prepared and handle conversations sensitively.

Another area in which your managers might need training is the selection of employees who will face redundancy. We will cover this subject further in

Chapter 6, but the managers are key to the selection process. They need to understand how to approach scoring the employees so that the selection produces the fairest results. They might need training in avoiding discrimination and unconscious bias. They might also benefit from training in how to manage difficult conversations. Each business is different, as is each manager within a business. Your decision on what training to include will depend on your own business.

The right mindset

The key to conveying the redundancy message compassionately and helpfully is for the person who is giving the message to be fully signed up to the decision beforehand. If a manager goes into a redundancy consultation meeting with the belief that the redundancy could have been avoided, the selection hasn't been fair or a negative view about any other aspect of the process, the person who is receiving the message will feel the negative energy and it will impact their reaction. Equally, if the manager is running the consultation simply because it is their job as a manager rather than because they have really understood why redundancies are happening, they will give out negative energy.

It is critical that managers are engaged in the redundancy planning and understand the need for the redundancy. They must be fully involved in the selection process (see Chapter 6) and feel confident that this is the correct outcome. That knowledge and confidence will give them the necessary mindset to help the redundant employee understand the situation. While the employee might not like the situation, they will be able to think more clearly about their future aspirations and goals and the steps needed to get there. How many times has an employee said that redundancy was the best thing that could have happened to them? It happens more often than you think, particularly when the manager giving the message has been able to help them to view it positively.

Having to be the message bearer can be a lonely and frightening place. The way to deal with that fear is to prepare well: managers should make sure they have run through what they need to say and they know the person who is receiving the message so that they have some positive things to say to them. Their confidence in the process will shine through.

There are some key so-called soft skills that successful managers need. Those skills are even more critical when it comes to giving the redundancy message. Managers must be able to listen to and hear the employee's thoughts and concerns. Managers must have empathy and be able to understand how the employee might be feeling (scared, anxious, worried, abandoned, discarded or unwanted; they may feel they are useless, lacking ability, too young, too old, too individual or don't fit in). When you are facing redundancy, it is easy to blame yourself. It is never your fault. The manager needs to help the individual understand that.

I promised redundancy, with love. If you love someone, you want the best for them and you want them to succeed. You put their needs before your own, celebrate their wins and console them when things aren't going well. You help them come to terms with and improve things. You listen to them, give them confidence and help them to shine. You are there for them when they need you. This is exactly what a leader should do for their team and what a manager should do when giving the redundancy message.

The final piece of the mindset puzzle is for managers to look after themselves. This is a stressful process and can be hard on them. They should make sure they take breaks, don't take it home with them and don't take things personally, even if the employee reacts badly and throws blame in their direction. It is not their fault any more than it is the employee's. Recognise that they might need some support as well. It is OK for managers to ask for help or to say they are finding it hard.

What support do managers need?

A big part of preparing managers to handle redundancy properly is making sure that they also get the support they need. If you are the business owner and will be managing the redundancies yourself, this includes you – we all need support when we are managing tricky situations.

The obvious support needed is training in the practicalities of redundancy such as the legalities, selecting the people affected, consulting with everyone and handling the dismissals. Part of this comes within a proper redundancy plan, which we have covered already and which your managers need to be familiar with, to make sure the facts are straight, the process has been fair and they have selected the right people.

Your managers are likely to find the process tough, especially if it is new to them or they do it infrequently. They might even be in a selection pool themselves, bringing a whole new level of stress. The well-being of the managers is important. They need time to prepare properly and they need to know how to get answers to their own questions and where to direct employees for answers to theirs. The more detailed your redundancy plan is, the more information is available to help everyone. Additionally, though, managers need somewhere to offload their feelings and emotions, particularly if a consultation meeting has proved difficult. You may need to provide access to counselling (for managers and employees alike) and it will be useful if managers have a peer group of other managers who are facing the same situations where they are safe to raise queries, concerns and suggestions.

Summary

In this chapter, we have covered the support and training that you and your managers might need to enable you to handle redundancies with compassion and kindness – both to the employees facing redundancy and to the managers themselves. Every piece of this redundancy puzzle is important to make the whole picture complete but getting this section right will help everything else fall into place.

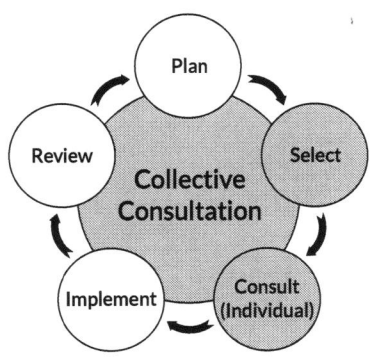

PART THREE
SELECTING AND CONSULTING

In this part, we get into the nuts and bolts of the redundancy process. Chapter 5 is about collective consultation. This process includes the entire workforce (or its representatives) and underpins the whole redundancy cycle. Chapter 6 is about selecting which employees will face the possibility of redundancy. It is critical that the selection is fair and transparent. In Chapter 7, we look at individual consultation with the people who have been identified by the selection process as likely to lose their jobs (that is, those who are 'at risk of redundancy').

How you handle these steps can make a huge difference to everyone concerned – including you – and the recovery and growth of the business in the future.

5
Select and Consult: Collective Consultation

Collective consultation – when an employer consults with representatives of its workforce about its redundancy plans – is at the centre of the redundancy cycle. From the planning stage right through to reviewing the process at the end, it is wise to keep collective consultation at the forefront. Some employers view collective consultation as merely a box to tick on the list of legal requirements. They are missing a trick and making the process much harder than it needs to be. Collective consultation is a chance to get valuable input and support from people who work closely with your employees and have their trust.

In this chapter, we are going to explore what collective consultation is, when we need to consult, whom we need to consult with and why. We will look in depth at what we need to consult about and we will also touch on the legalities.

Whom do we consult with and why?

Collective consultation is a legal requirement if you are going to make twenty or more people redundant within a ninety-day period.[26] It is good practice and I would advise you to consult collectively even if you have fewer than twenty redundancies. The consultation is completed with representatives of your workforce – recognised trade unions and/or employee representatives. If there aren't recognised trade unions representing every area of your workforce, you can consult with employee representatives elected by the workers in that area to represent their views in consultation and negotiations. Collective consultation might, therefore, purely be with trade union representatives, only with elected employee representatives or with a mixed body of both types of representatives.

It must be started early in the cycle. At the end of the planning stage, when you know what your redundancy process might look like, you should start to consult with the collective representatives about the details of what you are planning. The collective consultation should carry on until a way forward has been agreed upon, after which the individual consultations can start. In practice, though, it can be immensely helpful to continue with collective consultation throughout the whole process.

There are many reasons why collective consultation is a positive part of the process and helps employers to deal with redundancy with compassion and kindness:

1. It can help your employees to understand the business reasons for the redundancies and the alternatives you have considered.

2. The representatives provide a sounding-board for your reasons and plans and can often give an alternative viewpoint from an employee perspective.

3. It gives your employees a voice. In general terms, you get better engagement from employees if they feel heard. This is equally true in a redundancy situation if employees feel that their views and concerns have been raised by someone they trust.

4. The redundancy process is incredibly stressful for everyone concerned. Consulting both collectively and individually can help to reduce some of the stress and protect the well-being of everyone involved.

5. It can help you plan for the future of the business.

6. It might uncover ways to avoid redundancy altogether or reduce the need for so many redundancies.

7. It can improve communication with your employees.

8. It demonstrates openness and transparency, which builds trust with your employees.

9. For all the above reasons, if you are considering twenty or more redundancies, collective consultation is a legal requirement and failing to carry it out could lead to financial sanctions.

When I first started my HR career, the industrial relations landscape was about controversy, altercation and opposition. Over the years, it has evolved. Now, trade union representatives and employee representatives are more collaborative and act as partners trying to achieve a common goal. The key to successful collective consultation is to tap into the knowledge and skills of the representatives and engage with them to help to improve the redundancy process for everyone.

When consulting with employee representatives, it is important to be open to alternative suggestions and prepared to change your plans and approach. It is also useful to document any changes you make in light of their suggestions to ensure you have a record and in case your approach is challenged later.

When setting up the constitution/ground rules for your collective consultation body, consider the minimum number of managers and representatives needed for decisions. Timescales can easily slip when attendance is patchy or holidays and sickness intervene.

How long is the consultation and what do we need to consult about?

If there are twenty or more redundancies, the law is clear about when consultation must start (we will discuss this further later) but there is no prescribed duration for a consultation.[27] The important thing is that the consultation is meaningful. It is no good having a plan that is so rigid it cannot be changed. The purpose of the consultation is to get information and feedback from the representatives so they must be able to make counterproposals and suggestions, which must be given careful consideration and replies.

It can be difficult for employers to know how much information to share in collective consultation. You do not want to share commercially sensitive information that might give your competitors an advantage. I would suggest that employers share as much as possible to get the most out of the consultation otherwise your employees may feel that you are hiding something and mutual trust may suffer.

As a starting point, you must provide certain information in writing.[28] This includes the reasons for the redundancy, how many employees are affected, the categories of employees affected (including the number of employees in each category), how you are planning to select employees for redundancy, how you will carry out the redundancies, and details of how you will calculate redundancy payments.

If you want the consultation to be effective, helpful and meaningful, other information you might want to share is:

- Any support you hope to offer (eg outplacement or counselling).

- What, if any, alternative work you might be able to offer.

- A communications plan, including potential timescales, and what can and cannot be communicated and what is confidential.

- Ways of avoiding, reducing or mitigating redundancies that you have considered and why those alternatives have been rejected.

- What you plan to do about apprentices, interns, contractors and agency staff.

The representatives might have views and ideas about the above information and this can be helpful for your planning.

I would also suggest that you start a question-and-answer (Q&A) document that can be shared with employees so they can see what the consultations have covered. This will probably change and grow throughout the consultation. It is helpful if any new questions raised are referred back to the consultation body for an agreed and consistent answer.

If you care about your employees, you need to be open to counterproposals from the representatives. Consider any such proposals carefully and respond fully. This can be time-consuming but it is well worth doing as it can help the employees who will be affected (both those leaving and those left behind) come to terms with the situation and understand the reasoning behind it.

Form filling and legalities

There are legal guidelines that you must follow if you want to avoid ending up at an employment tribunal. While there is no time limit on how long consultations must last, there is a minimum period before you can dismiss any employees (depending on the number of redundancies). If you are planning between twenty and ninety-nine redundancies (including volunteers and redeployments), the minimum consultation period before dismissal is thirty days. This timescale increases for a higher number of redundancies. When planning 100 or more redundancies, the minimum consultation period is forty-five days.[29]

For twenty or more redundancies, you must also inform the government that you will be making redundancies so that the government can provide help to your redundant employees. The information is shared with Jobcentre Plus and any government training agencies. You must use a specific form (HR1) to notify the redundancy payments service (RPS).

There are specific timescales for this depending on the number of proposed redundancies.[30] For between twenty and ninety-nine proposed redundancies, you must notify the RPS at least thirty days before the first redundancy and, if you are anticipating 100 or more redundancies, it must be done forty-five days before the first redundancy. If you don't notify the RPS, you could be fined an unlimited amount.

When planning fewer than twenty redundancies, there are no legal restrictions and you do not have to go through collective consultation. In practice, though, you may want to take advantage of the benefits that collective consultation can bring.

Summary

If you are planning twenty or more redundancies, there are legal requirements that you must fulfil, including collective consultation with trade union or employee representatives. This can seem onerous and time-consuming but there are huge advantages to partnering with these representatives and tapping into their knowledge and relationship with your employees.

Collective consultation can help reduce the stress involved in redundancy planning. The representatives are there to speak on behalf of the employees but they are a step removed from the personal reactions that can come out in individual consultation. They will help enormously with creating a workable, fair and compassionate redundancy plan and process. They are also invaluable in communicating with the affected employees.

6
Select and Consult: Selection

How do you make sure you choose the 'right' people for redundancy? The short answer is that you can't. There is no 'right' person who deserves to be selected for redundancy. Nobody deserves to lose their job because their employer is in financial difficulties or needs to cut costs.

You may have someone who is not performing their job well or barely sticks to the rules. Perhaps someone upsets their colleagues or is rude to clients or you, their boss. Maybe there is someone who is always off sick so you wouldn't miss them anyway. Surely one of these employees would be the right person to make redundant? No, as it happens. None of these is a good – or even acceptable – reason to select someone for redundancy. There are well-trodden paths for dealing with each of those issues. The only fair way to choose is to mark every eligible employee against objective selection criteria. That is what we are going to explore in this chapter.

Guidelines for selection criteria

It is useful to start from the base that all of your employees are worth keeping. After all, you have invested a great deal of time and money in them and you want to select the best employees to remain in the organisation. Your selection should be focused on future skills you need or the right experience to drive your business forward, and not necessarily on performance, conduct or ability. The employees who are made redundant are going to face a tough time – you don't want to add to that by making them feel that they have been selected for being the worst performers. It is more uplifting for everyone if you select the people who are best placed to stay. This may just be a nuance in your thinking but I can guarantee it will lead to happier results.

There are other routes for dealing with the various difficult issues that I referred to in the introduction to this chapter. Disciplinary procedures deal with performance or conduct and there are ways to address conflict such as mediation. You can move someone who is rude to clients to a role that is not client-facing. You can have a 'difficult conversation' with or even take disciplinary action against someone who is rude to the boss and attendance processes deal with excessive sickness. These issues are not reasons to select someone for redundancy.

There are many, varied ways to select which employees should be made redundant. You want to ensure your process will select the people you can most afford to lose. There are always risks in the selection and you want to ensure you avoid any claims of discrimination. It is a potential minefield and you need to be fair and transparent.

The only fair way to select employees for redundancy is to mark them against objective selection criteria. Those criteria might include some of the difficult issues already mentioned such as having an outstanding warning for performance or misconduct or for high levels of absence (although care is needed to avoid discriminating against disabled or pregnant people). It might be better not to use the criteria to select the poorest performing people for redundancy. You might find it more effective to use the criteria to select for retention the people who are most aligned with your business goals and aspirations.

You are likely to have a plan for where you want the business to be in one, three or five years. If your business has suffered financially (which may be the reason you are contemplating redundancies), you may need to change direction, look at new technologies, consider different markets or produce different products.

Once you know where you want to be in the future, you can determine the skills, experience and knowledge you need to get there. Have you got those in the workplace already? What soft skills will your employees need? What will your new teams look like? You can then place those skills, knowledge and experience high on the list of your selection criteria.

Next, the list of criteria might include aptitude and attitude towards gaining those skills. You may want to add criteria like performance, conduct and attendance but take care as there is the potential to discriminate (indirectly and unwittingly) against people with particular protected characteristics (disability, part-time, age, etc). Whatever criteria you use must be fair and measurable (as far as possible). To be as fair and transparent as possible, consult with your employee representatives and recognised trade unions about the criteria. Once you have agreed your selection criteria, you use them to score people in your selection pools.

Selection is one of the most important parts of the redundancy process. It can easily go wrong and lead to legal difficulties if you have not taken care to avoid discrimination or personal bias in the process.

Selection pools and scoring

If you have more than one role at risk of redundancy, you will need to consider selection pools.[31] A selection pool is needed where more than one person is doing the same or similar work. For example, if you have several retail workers and you want to reduce the number by one, you need a selection pool of retail workers. All of your retail workers go into that pool. Each is assessed against the same selection criteria and the person who scores the highest (or lowest depending on how your selection criteria work) is the one likely to be made redundant.

The question is whom to include in each pool. You will need to look broadly across the organisation to identify all the jobs that require the same skills you are reducing. For example, in the retail workers pool you might want to include someone who only does retail to internal customers. The role and skills are the same for all retail workers – only the clients are different. Anybody doing those jobs has to be included in the selection pool and your collective consultation representatives must cover those areas as well. If you have retail managers, should they go in the same pool? Probably not, as they are not doing the same job (although some elements may overlap). If you also needed to reduce the retail managers, there would be a separate pool of retail managers.

Before setting up a selection pool, check any agreements in your redundancy policy or that you have made with a recognised trade union. If there is no existing policy or agreement, it is sensible to consult with any recognised trade union or employee representatives about how the selection pools should be arranged. It is important that all people in the same or similar roles, with the same skills, are selected using the same criteria. Then all of your employees can see that the selection has been made fairly. They may not like the situation, but they will feel more comfortable with it.

Determining eligible employees (the 'pools' of people affected) is no easy task. The general rule is to think broadly about which groups of employees should be included. It is all too easy to exclude particular groups early on only to find that the fairness of your process is challenged later. In that case, this early step would need to be repeated with all the angst that correcting the previous communications might involve. There is a balance to be struck; you want to avoid telling employees that they are at risk of redundancy unnecessarily.

Once your pools are set up, apply the chosen selection criteria to everyone in the pool. Some – or all – of the criteria can be used for each selection pool. There may need to be differences if certain jobs have specific skill requirements but, in the main, they can be fairly generic. The selection criteria should be explained to everyone so they understand exactly how the selection is made. The agreed criteria give you a good base from which to answer questions consistently and fairly.

Scoring can be carried out in a variety of ways, as long as it is transparent and consistent. You could award points for criteria that must be met, such as good performance, having skills needed in the future and good attendance. In this scenario, the lowest-scoring people will be at risk of redundancy. Alternatively, you can award points for undesirable factors such as a disciplinary record, poor attendance or poor performance. In that case, the highest-scoring employees will be at risk of redundancy.

Either method is fine as long as it is clear and there is a fair measure of the points. When it comes to the second method, take care though – you can only give points for poor performance or poor conduct if the person is aware that their performance or conduct was not good (ie if some action has been taken against them or their appraisal was poor). If attendance is among your criteria, you must ignore any absence due to disability, maternity or pregnancy.

Objective, accurate data and documentation are crucial to back up your selection scores. Those selected may ask to see others' scores. You must not breach confidentiality by sharing someone else's scores but you may be able to share anonymised, average scores if you want to do so. It may be better to avoid sharing any information about scores as those who score below the average can feel undervalued or even aggrieved.

Careful consideration

There are specific groups of people who you may need to consider carefully to avoid putting them at a disadvantage. They include those who are pregnant and on maternity leave, people on long-term absence for another reason, disabled employees, people who have caring responsibilities and part-time employees.

Let us look first at the issue of pregnancy or maternity. Employers often think that employees who are pregnant or on maternity leave must be left out of any consideration for redundancy but that is not fair to all of the other people in a selection pool. It is perfectly lawful to consider these employees for redundancy but it must be done fairly and within certain parameters.

Here is a brief overview of the law regarding redundancy for pregnant employees and those on maternity leave:[32]

- Redundancy must be genuine and necessary.

- You must consult and keep in touch with them even if they are on maternity leave. You must make sure they are aware of any changes at work so they are not disadvantaged. Failure to consult with a pregnant employee on maternity leave is likely to be considered unfair discrimination.

- You must use redundancy selection criteria that do not discriminate. You *cannot* use pregnancy or maternity leave as a reason to dismiss someone – this is automatically unfair dismissal as well as unlawful discrimination.

- You must consider alternative work and the employee must be given preference over other workers. She must be offered an alternative role if there is one – she doesn't have to apply for it.

- You may find during an employee's maternity leave that you can manage without her by redistributing or reorganising the work. This is not a valid reason to make her redundant. An employee on maternity leave has the right to return to her job, even if you have employed a temporary replacement who is better at the job.

- Pregnant women may need more stringent health and safety measures. This is not a good (or safe) reason to select them for redundancy.

In addition to direct discrimination, there is a risk that the selection criteria used for redundancy may indirectly discriminate. For example, if attendance or performance is included as a criterion for selecting who should be made redundant, an employee who is pregnant or has been on maternity leave might score higher so maternity-related absence should not be included.

At the time of writing, the proposed Pregnancy and Maternity (Redundancy Protection) Bill is going through government consultation.[33] The bill proposes to prohibit a woman from being made redundant from the start of the pregnancy until six months after returning to work except in certain circumstances. This is not yet in force but it may be passed into law in the future.

Another group that needs careful consideration are those with caring responsibilities. They are more likely to work part-time and they can be overlooked. They likely have to be strict about start and finish times to fit in with their caring responsibilities and they are more likely to ask for flexible working of some kind. They should not be marked down for these factors, but it is easy to forget to make allowances for individual circumstances when you are scoring against specific criteria. The selection criteria and scoring method need careful thought to avoid unintentional discrimination.

Disabled people can also face a disadvantage when scored against selection criteria. In particular, if attendance is being considered, it must not include any disability-related absence. When performance is measured, you must make sure that there is a level bar. Mental health issues can be exacerbated by the anxiety of potential or pending redundancy. Concern about getting another job is likely to be greater for someone who is facing time out of the workplace because of a disability.

You may not know whether your employees have any mental health issues or other disabilities. Bear in mind that there could be an invisible health issue or 'hidden disability' that people want to keep private. Statistically, one in four faces mental health challenges in the workplace each year so some of your employees likely fall into that category.[34]

If you know about any disability (or you are made aware of it during the redundancy programme), you are not prevented from carrying on with the redundancy but you must handle it with care (and love, of course).

Here is a list of things to consider when scoring those with disabilities:

- When scoring for selection purposes, think carefully about any adjustment you need to make for the disability.

- You may need to have more consultation meetings than you envisaged. You may have to repeat the messages. You may want to allow the employee to be accompanied at consultation meetings even when this is not by the normal work colleague or TU representative. There may be a requirement for an interpreter and this is a legal right.

- The fact that someone needs potentially expensive or complex adjustments to enable them to continue working is not a good (or fair or lawful) reason for selecting them for redundancy.

- Ask the individual if there is any particular help or support they need.

- Think about other support you might be able to provide such as counselling, referral to occupational health professionals, career coaching, outplacement or financial advice.

Employers need to avoid unfair selection for redundancy (for example, because someone was judged on performance or attendance during a period of disability-related sickness or shielding). It is important to avoid automatically unfair reasons for redundancy (for example, if a disabled person complained about a lack of safety or denial of reasonable adjustments) and discrimination (they were not offered the option of an alternative suitable job, for instance).[35]

Disabled people are already disadvantaged in the job market (although this had been improving before the pandemic). They find it much harder to get work and they are twice as likely as nondisabled workers to be still unemployed after twelve months.[36] Redundancy is potentially even more challenging for a disabled worker than for others in employment. It is in the hands of business owners and leaders to help to make the world a fairer place for them.

Another sector of workers that you may need to consider carefully is BAME employees. If you have followed previous advice, your criteria will be fair on the face of it but always double-check whether they could have a disproportionate effect on BAME employees. Sadly, due to years of discrimination, BAME employees are likely to be less qualified, have less experience and have missed out on training opportunities. They are likely to have started later in your employment. This means that they would score higher in some of the standard selection criteria used in redundancy programmes. You may need to adjust the scoring process to take into account these disadvantages.

My advice is not to make assumptions and instead check for any likely disproportionate effect before you start scoring. Adjust the scoring system accordingly if necessary but only if it is an issue for your organisation. Estimating is likely to be incorrect and lead to unfairness. The point is to be as fair, objective and transparent as possible throughout your whole redundancy programme.

When you have scored people against the criteria, I advise you to have the scores checked independently by another manager to ensure the scoring has not been influenced by unconscious bias. This is what redundancy, with love, looks like.

Volunteers

There may be those in your organisation who would welcome the chance to take a redundancy package and move on to other opportunities. It may seem the obvious solution – you can cut roles without making people leave unless they want to.

It is never as simple as that:

1. The volunteers may not be in the roles that need to be cut. The people who *are* in those roles may not have the aptitude and ability to move into the jobs left open by the volunteers.

2. Volunteers for redundancy often do so because they are confident in their ability to get another role. This probably means they are your best people, are in hard-to-fill roles or have niche skills that you might struggle to replace.

3. Some people volunteer for redundancy because they have calculated that their redundancy package will be substantial. They see it as an easy way to get a large sum of money. This means that they are probably among the employees who will cost you the most in terms of redundancy pay.

4. Volunteers may be the people who least need training and development so you may still have a large training cost to upskill others who remain.

On the other hand, there might be occasions when accepting volunteers for redundancy is the best option for your company. It is wise to give careful consideration to whether or not you open your redundancy selection to volunteers. If you ask for volunteers but decide not to allow those volunteers to leave, you will have unhappy employees to contend with. The volunteers who can't leave will be disgruntled and may start looking for other roles anyway. The people who end up facing redundancy despite others having volunteered may be frustrated and raise a legal challenge against you.

If you decide that you do want to permit volunteers, you might want to consider offering an enhanced redundancy payment to anyone who volunteers. This can encourage people to volunteer and mean that others who want to stay with you will not be at risk.

THE GIFT OF POSITIVITY

I was a shy and gawky young girl. I could usually be found with my head in a book – or the clouds. I hated sports lessons. I was always the last to be picked to join a team. Not because I was unpopular but because I had two left feet and could be relied on to drop the ball, miss a catch or run in the wrong direction. I wanted to fit in. I wanted to be the one who was picked first.

Later, during my working life, I took voluntary redundancy from my job. It was my choice –

I volunteered. Even so, I had that familiar feeling of rejection from my childhood. I wanted them to say, 'No, you can't possibly leave, we need you too much.' I sometimes wonder if that is why I volunteered – so I wouldn't be the one who was selected; so I wouldn't be made to feel that I wasn't good enough.

Redundancy is hard, even for the volunteers. Nobody wants to be the one left standing alone when the teams have been chosen. If you handle it well, you can give the gift of hope and positivity to those facing redundancy.

Summary

In this chapter, we have looked at how to select which employees will face redundancy. It is critical that you get this right. The selection process must be fair and transparent so that everyone affected can see how the decisions have been made. This will help those facing redundancy to accept the difficult situation they are in and it will also help those who remain in the business to see that the process has been handled fairly and consistently.

7
Select and Consult: Individual Consultation

Having completed the selection process, it is time to move on to individual consultation. This is the part of the cycle that managers often find most daunting.

In this chapter, we are going to look at why individual consultation is important, what to cover and how to make it easier for everyone involved. We will consider who can accompany the individual during the consultation and who should not be allowed to be involved. We will look at what reactions you can expect from employees facing redundancy and how to deal with them. Finally, and most importantly, we will think about the best ways to approach these conversations and the skills that managers need to effectively navigate this part of the process.

What is the point of individual consultation?

Both managers and individuals find the need to consult about redundancy difficult. The decision has been made that redundancy needs to happen, for whatever reason (usually money), so what is the point of consulting about it? Surely it just prolongs the agony for everyone – why is it a legal requirement?

There are good reasons to consult with employees on an individual basis:

- The consultation might uncover a way to avoid redundancy altogether.

- It can enable suggestions and requests that might have been overlooked.

- It gives the employee the chance to air their feelings, let off steam and think about how best to handle their situation.

- It can change the employee's selection scoring (although this is a double-edged sword and can be a disadvantage if it puts someone else at risk in their place).

- It gives managers a chance to provide real support and leadership and to help the employee understand why this situation has arisen. Employees may not like it but they will at least feel the process has been fair, they have had the chance to raise their concerns and it is not their fault.

• It can help defend a legal challenge.

Consultation is not just a hurdle to overcome before redundancy is finalised. It can change things significantly – but it must be genuine and meaningful. A manager with the mindset that 'it's a done deal' can give the impression that the consultation is not genuine. Those affected will quickly realise this and may be more likely to raise grievances.

Fair redundancy processes and procedures are critical to helping protect employees and employers alike. Someone may not currently be at work – they may be on maternity or paternity leave, long-term sick leave or sabbatical – but that doesn't negate the need for proper consultation. Consultation ensures that those with specific support needs (such as disabled employees or carers) can discuss them. It allows the employer to make clear the reasons for redundancy and for the selection of that individual in particular. Consultation can be done remotely – there is nothing that says it must be done in person – although that can bring its own challenges. It may be more difficult to gauge reactions or get any input (but that can be difficult in person too).

It is kinder, safer and better for an ongoing employment relationship and employer reputation to consult with the individuals, hear what they have to say and seriously explore ways to avoid redundancy.

Being accompanied

Interestingly, the law only provides for employees to be accompanied at a disciplinary or grievance hearing.[37] When you consult with employees on an individual basis, there is no legal right to be accompanied. In practice, it is the norm for employees to be allowed a companion who is normally a work colleague or trade union representative, as specified for disciplinary and grievance hearings.

In my experience, employees facing redundancy often ask to be accompanied by a different companion outside of these parameters such as a family member or a friend, or sometimes they ask for a legal representative. I have been asked if someone could have an external redundancy consultant attend with them. It might seem the kind thing is to allow them to be accompanied by whomever they choose. They are going through a tough time and, naturally, a caring manager wants the individual to feel as comfortable as possible. My advice is to stick to the legal guidelines that are in place for other processes and only allow a work colleague or trade union representative to accompany an employee.

There is a reason why the legislation and Acas guidelines regarding disciplinary and grievance hearings specify a work colleague or trade union representative only: it protects the company and the individual.[38] The most frequent request is to be accompanied by a legal representative. Redundancy is complicated and people are aware that there are legislative rules. They can be afraid that they do not know enough about the law and want to be accompanied by someone with legal training. That often applies to the manager giving the message as well. It is a difficult message to give and managers are often concerned that they might make a slip-up that causes legal repercussions. If one party has a legal representative present, it is only fair that the other party does also and then you could find yourself in a situation where the case is argued on legal grounds as if you were in a court or tribunal. Before you know it, the case has escalated into a legal battle and the point of the consultation (to support the employee) has been lost.

You might ask, 'What about an employee's mother or neighbour?' The same problem arises – someone's mother might be a trained and practising lawyer. In any event, she is not going to be impartial and fair. This can potentially turn a consultation into a battle, which is not helpful for either party.

As always, judge each case on its merits. If your employee is eighteen or younger, having a parent present might be helpful to everyone.

WHAT NOT TO DO

Let me tell you about the time I mistakenly allowed an external redundancy consultant to accompany someone in a redundancy consultation.

It was a difficult situation in which the person (who was a trade union member) was turned down by the union. The union did not want to accompany the individual as, when they had done so in the past, the employee had disregarded their advice. The employee did not have any close working colleagues and felt nobody could be trusted as a companion. I felt sorry for the employee (never a good basis for a decision of this nature) and, as I had confidence in my redundancy knowledge, I was prepared to allow an external redundancy consultant.

During the consultation, the external consultant was voluble and argumentative. He did not help his client's cause and made the meeting more difficult for the employee's manager. It turned out that – based on the employee's inaccurate briefing – he had told the employee that he would be able to prevent the redundancy. The employee was even more upset when that proved impossible. The situation was more unpleasant for everyone than it might have been and I regretted my impulse to bend the rules because of misplaced sympathy.

What the individual consultation should cover

Individual consultation can have such a huge impact on the individual and their future. The main aim of the consultation is to enable the employee to understand the position the company is in, what alternatives have been considered and why redundancies are the only answer. They also need to understand how they have been selected to lose their job. They are likely to believe that it is their fault. A big part of the manager's role in the consultation is to reassure the individual that they have not brought this upon themselves.

The consultation has to cover the changes that are needed in the company and how that has led to redundancies. It should also cover the selection process and how the individual has arrived at this point. The person must be given a chance to air their views about how the selection has happened and whether they think it has been fair or not. They need to feel their points have been heard.

They must also have the chance to suggest ways they can avoid redundancy. In most cases, that can either mean that the selection needs to be reviewed, which may – or may not – mean the employee's score changes (and someone else would face redundancy) or that they are interested in another role within the company. If there are any other possible roles the employee could do, they must be discussed – even if they involve working from a different site or on less favourable terms. It is good practice to circulate all vacancies to those selected and to follow up in individual consultation meetings to obtain the employee's reaction.

You also need to cover any potential help that the company can offer to the individual – CV writing, outplacement support, job search, training, or financial and other counselling. These options are covered in more detail elsewhere in this book but there is likely something that can be done to help to lessen the blow.

The most obvious way for an employee to avoid redundancy is to accept other work within the company – a so-called 'suitable alternative'.[39] In legal terms, this means that if there are any vacancies that the employee might have the skills, experience and interest to fulfil, you have to offer them the chance to get that role. For a role to be considered a suitable alternative, the salary must be similar and the employee must meet the basic requirements of the job. They might have skills and experience that are currently unused (and so you do not know about them) and they might be prepared to change track to remain employed. My advice is to talk about any vacancies you have (even if they do not seem 'suitable') as the employee might be interested. If they are interested and want to apply, you should interview them. If they do not get the job, they should be given feedback on why they were unsuccessful. If an employee takes a suitable alternative, it will be on a month's trial basis. If it does not work out during that month, the redundancy can go ahead instead.[40]

Additionally, if the employee is on maternity leave, she *must* be offered any suitable alternative role even if you do not think she is the best person for it.[41] If she has the skills it requires, the job is hers – she does not have to apply or interview, she must just be offered the role.[42]

You can meet with the individual as many times as necessary for the consultation to be completed. If the person is upset or in denial (and I talk more about reactions later in this chapter), you may need to meet more than once. The employee needs to feel they have had every chance to raise their concerns and questions and to get answers. Even if you only have one meeting, my advice is to keep the door open for them to request another or to raise any queries as the process carries on. The aim is that they feel they have been heard, their views have been considered, their questions answered and they have received adequate support and help. There is no set timescale for the consultation. It must be as long as is necessary and this will vary from person to person.

You will eventually need to bring an end to the consultation. Once you have answered everything they have raised and explained the process fully, that is long enough. You might see instances in which employees try to spin out the consultation to delay the inevitable end of their employment. You need to feel confident you have covered everything and given them every opportunity to provide input and then wrap it up, even if they resist. It is kinder in the long run to bring the consultation to an end than to keep an open-ended discussion going. Recruitment freezes and vacancy approvals are important tools to manage the process and prevent consultation from being extended on the basis that a vacancy might arise in the future.

BRINGING THE CONSULTATION TO AN END

Years ago, I supported a manager in an organisation that had decided to restructure its business. For sound business reasons, it intended to stop doing a particular type of work that was not central to its business and did not fit its future direction. This meant that those doing that work were no longer required. The individuals were each told about the proposed changes and were given a clear written statement describing the reasoning behind the decision.

One of the employees doing the job found it difficult to accept the situation. She tried to overturn the decision to close down the relevant part of the business. The process kept being delayed because she failed to attend consultation meetings, often taking sickness absence the day before or the day of the consultation meetings. She did not wish to engage with the consultation about the proposed redundancy, alternative roles or the other support the organisation might have been able to offer. Eventually, there was no option but to complete the consultation in writing, ensuring that she was provided with the opportunity to respond and discuss, and an appeal process.

The final matter to raise in connection with consultation is the right of appeal. Even if there is no mechanism in your redundancy process for an appeal (and I suggest that you should have an appeal process), employees have the right to raise a complaint about their redundancy if they feel the process was unfair or they were unfairly selected.[43] It is much easier if there is a specific route to appeal which is made clear to the employee during the consultation. Without it, they are likely to feel you are hiding something. It is also a good way to bring the consultation to an end – if they insist they have more to consult about but you cannot get to the bottom of any serious issues, then offering an appeal leaves them an avenue to raise any concerns.

Individual consultation checklist

There is a checklist of areas to cover during an individual consultation below. For all areas, you should ensure the employee understands the situation and its implications for them. Be clear that the discussion is confidential and that (for instance) selection scoring will not be shared with others. Allow comfort breaks, if needed, and time to compose him/herself if the employee gets upset.

At any stage, you can agree to go away and reflect on what has been said and meet again at another date to give an answer (eg if the selection scores need to be reviewed). You do not need to answer every question immediately – it is always better to go away and check if you are unsure of anything.

You may not cover everything on the checklist in one meeting. If the employee raises questions or suggestions, it might be necessary to hold one or more further meetings until everything has been covered properly.

✓ Check the employee knows they are entitled to be accompanied by a trade union representative or work colleague (or an agreed companion, eg if employee is disabled and needs specific support).

✓ Cover the reasons that led to the need for the redundancies – ensure employee understands.

✓ Cover alternatives to redundancy that have been considered and reasons for their rejection.

✓ If there has been a selection, ensure employee understands the process of selection.

✓ Share the individual's scores (but not those of others in the pool) and why those scores have been given.

✓ Give the employee the chance to comment on their scores and listen to any representations they make. You may need to change the scoring accordingly.

✓ Listen to any views the employee has about how to avoid redundancy – they might come up with something that you have not thought of.

✓ Discuss available roles elsewhere in the organisation, whether or not they might be suitable and if the employee wants to apply. Keep an open mind – they know their skills and experience; you may not know everything. Allow them to apply for other jobs if possible. Explain the trial period for a suitable alternative role and that they can still take redundancy and get redundancy pay if it does not work out.

✓ If an employee is on maternity leave, you must offer her any suitable alternative role which is available. She does not have to apply or interview.

✓ Cover any help the company can offer – outplacement services, CV writing, time off to look for alternative work, training support, counselling, financial advice, etc.

✓ Share potential redundancy pay figures (subject to a final date being confirmed) – they can find it useful to know roughly how much money to expect.

✓ Check whether they have any more questions or comments or want to discuss anything else.

✓ Confirm that you are available whenever they need you to answer any further questions or to have further discussions.

✓ Confirm when next meeting will be (or that there will not be one if everything has been covered sufficiently).

✓ Confirm what happens next (eg further meeting or letter to confirm their redundancy). Confirm potential final date of employment if known.

✓ Advise that, if their redundancy is confirmed, they will have the right to appeal against the decision.

If you want the employee to sign a settlement agreement, you may also need to discuss this during the consultation and explain what that means, why you are suggesting it and what benefits it has for them.[44]

Ensure you take notes of all points discussed and any questions raised. Respond to questions within a reasonable timeframe (say five days) or at the next consultation meeting (and confirm when that will be).

HOW NOT TO DO IT

I met someone recently whose son had been made redundant. He was called to a consultation meeting about redundancy. He was not offered the chance to be accompanied at the meeting. It turned out that it was not a consultation – he was made redundant during that meeting.

The company had gone through a selection process to decide who would be made redundant but he was not allowed to see his scores, so he had no idea why he had been selected. When he said that he wanted to appeal his redundancy, he was told that the decision had been made and he could not do so.

The final date of his employment was two days before he would have become entitled to a redundancy payment (ie two years' employment at the company). The individual thought that the company avoided the consultation stage so that they could end his employment before they had to pay him anything. Even if that was not the case, an employment tribunal hearing would need to see evidence from the company to prove that and the denial of an appeal could be considered an unfair process. It could potentially cost the company far more money than it would save in redundancy pay if that was indeed their motive.

Reactions

Millions of us have had to go through redundancy, some more than once. That includes me. Let me tell you – it stinks! Even if you volunteered or received a decent payout, you can feel rejected, undervalued, unloved or even worthless. If you are resilient, these feelings may pass quickly and the situation might turn into an opportunity to move on to greater things but, at that moment when you know your turn has come, it hurts.

How your redundancy is managed by your employer is critical to how quickly you bounce back. Getting it right does not need to cost a business much financially but it can make a huge difference to the employees on the receiving end – and the business as well.

I have supported employers with redundancy programmes for over two decades, and I have seen a huge variety of reactions from employees when they face the news. It is not possible to guess or predict the emotions someone else will feel when they are dealing with redundancy.

Redundancy can feel like bereavement and the individual needs to grieve. Even if it is voluntary, it can still engender a feeling of loss. It is a frightening time for many people. They worry about finding another job, especially when many others are job seeking at the same time. Often, there are money worries. A redundancy payment only goes so far and it is often nowhere near the amount people are expecting.

Those who lose their jobs – through no fault of their own – may feel a sense of failure. They wonder if they could have somehow prevented it, especially if they have been through a selection process and scored lower than some of their peers. They might feel shame and dread the reaction of family and friends. Some feel anger born of fear. They feel they have been let down by the company and their hard work has gone unrecognised. They might threaten legal action.

Denial is another reaction you may get in redundancy consultations. As it is such a challenging discussion to have, it has been known for managers to turn the bad news into such a light conversation that the selected employee does not realise they have been made redundant.

DEALING WITH DENIAL

I once worked with a company that asked me to sit in on all of their individual redundancy consultation meetings. My presence gave the managers confidence and I could make sure that nothing important was missed.

We met with one young employee who didn't have any questions or anything to say at the meeting. He clearly just wanted to leave. The day after his leaving date, he turned up for work as normal. He had failed to take in (or face up to) the loss of his job.

Denial is a fairly common response to a redundancy consultation. People don't want to accept the bad news and they might not take it in. In this case, the manager was shocked and upset and I felt that I had failed the individual who was facing redundancy, the company and the manager.

I learnt a valuable lesson from this dreadful episode. I have seen denial as a response to redundancy many times since and I am much more alert to it and deal with it sympathetically.

Occasionally someone is happy about the situation. Maybe they have other plans for their future and were only hanging on at work in the hope of redundancy pay. These are the employees who might volunteer for redundancy but they may also be your best workers who have no fears about finding other work. Most people feel a mixture of different emotions. Some people may not show their emotions or they may stifle their natural reactions.

A manager might see some or all of these different reactions to redundancy. My experience is that a redundancy consultation is among the most difficult conversations a manager can have with their team members. Nobody wants to give bad news and the manager is probably dreading the meeting and might be apprehensive about the reaction they will get.

The manager is also likely to have built a relationship with the employee. They may be grieving the loss of a good employee or concerned about whether the employee will find another job. They will worry about future team dynamics without that individual. There could be concerns about how the work will be distributed. What can be changed or stopped so that the remaining team can function? What about the people who survive the redundancy and remain in the company – how are they going to feel?

Teams will be concerned about the future workload following redundancy. How will the redundant employee's work be resourced? Will they need more training? If so, some may be happy; others may worry. People will also be grieving the loss of a colleague – a familiar face no longer there. Some will be friendly with the departed person and feel aggrieved on behalf of their friend. Others may be relieved that a difficult colleague has left. Alternatively, if they have been involved in a selection process, the overwhelming reaction might be relief that their job is safe. Some may even feel superior and falsely proud that they scored highly enough to stay. Some may be frustrated because they would have liked to leave with the benefit of a redundancy payment.

In some cases, the manager may be concerned about their own role. Their job might also be at risk of redundancy or they may be concerned that it is going to happen to them soon. If the company is in such dire straits that it is making jobs redundant, can it survive? Will their job be safe?

There are others who may have reactions to and feelings about redundancy: for example, customers and clients of the company, particularly if the redundant employee was client-facing. Suppliers may also have a relationship with specific employees. These people's reactions also affect your business and you may need to manage the message to them.

When companies are planning for redundancies, they might find it helpful to think about all of the potential reactions and how to deal with them. This will help the business to quickly get back to productivity following the redundancy programme.

The personal touch

From the moment people are told they are at risk of redundancy they are in a state of shock. Some may get over that fairly quickly and be able to deal with the situation. Others may remain in shock throughout the whole process and beyond. The biggest gift a manager can give them is time. They need time to take in the message, which may need to be repeated several times, and time to come to terms with it. Try to think about how they might be feeling, their fears and anxieties. They are likely to feel it is somehow their fault and they could have prevented it. They will almost certainly have questions. Empathy and patience are the two biggest skills you, as the manager, will need.

Over the years, I have found that the things people appreciate most are honesty, clarity and consistency. They like to feel they are being treated professionally. They need to feel safe to air their feelings and concerns without fear of the consequences, so the consultation meeting/s should take place where you will not be interrupted, overheard or seen. They will not feel comfortable if their reactions can be seen by others.

If there has been a selection process and you are giving feedback on their score and the reasons for it, it is helpful to stick to the facts and not embellish or cover up the truth. Try to relate the feedback to the specific behaviour you have witnessed so that they can understand how it has affected the scoring. This is why the scoring must be based on real and measurable aspects of the role, and not just on your feelings. They may ask to know what others have scored and you need to make it clear that you cannot share that information with them.

Try to avoid too much small talk to put the person at ease. They will appreciate a more direct approach as long as it is non-judgemental and clear and they can relate it to their own view of things. Try not to make things personal or about their attitude or character, but rather focus on behaviour. Don't beat about the bush for fear of offending or upsetting the individual. They are likely to be upset anyway and they will feel worse if you do not provide a straight answer. Your role is to help them to understand why they are in this position so that they can come to terms with it.

The way I have always approached this is to imagine what the other person is going through and how difficult this process is for them. If you can put yourself in their place for a few minutes, it can help you to know how best to approach the conversation.

It is unlikely that you will come away from the consultation feeling it has gone well and you have handled it perfectly. You are only human and it is a hard thing to do. The important thing is to keep the door open for more discussion and you will find it gets easier as the person comes to terms with their situation. Focusing on the future and possible opportunities, next steps, help available and key dates can be helpful to avoid a preoccupation with the past or facts and decisions that are unlikely to be changed.

Consulting with volunteers for redundancy

If someone has volunteered for redundancy, there is only the need for minimal consultation. They have not been through a selection process so there is no scoring to explain and discuss. It is worth having a conversation to make sure they have no unanswered questions. Normally, once they have expressed their interest in voluntary redundancy, the company will send out the offer, including the financial terms and any other applicable information, and there is no further need for consultation once the volunteer has accepted the offer.

In the case of voluntary redundancy, the dates (when their notice starts, if applicable, and when their employment ends) included in the redundancy offer are contractual and can only be changed by mutual agreement. Both parties have to abide by the terms offered. This differs from compulsory redundancy, where the company can rescind the position at the last minute. If it is rescinded, I still advise consultation to avoid having a disgruntled employee who was not expecting to remain in your employment. Some employees may be relieved but an employee who has already come to terms with the redundancy and made plans for the future might not welcome an eleventh-hour change of position.

Summary

In this chapter, we have looked at individual consultation and how to make it professional and as helpful as possible for the individual. We have considered why we need to consult individually and what we need to cover during the consultation. We have looked at the individual's right to be accompanied and whom they can choose as a companion. Finally, we have considered some of the best ways to approach the conversation. In many ways, this is the most important chapter in the book as the consultation has the greatest impact on the individual by giving them the chance to air their concerns and feelings and come to terms with their new future.

PART FOUR
MAKING IT HAPPEN

Having selected which individuals will face redundancy and consulted with the workforce representatives and the affected individuals, we now reach the part of the process where the redundancy happens and people start to leave your employment.

In this section, we look at their final days of employment and what help you might offer them as they move forward into a different life. We will also consider the financial support that you can and should give them.

8
Implement: Notice

Assuming that the redundancy is going ahead, once the individual consultation is complete it is time to look at the dismissal process. The first thing to do is to give the employee written notice that their employment will end due to redundancy. During their notice period, your support and help can make a difference. If you get it right, the employee will leave on good terms and your reputation as a good employer will not be tarnished.

What does the contract say?

As with any termination of employment, it is important to check what the individual terms and conditions of employment say regarding the notice period. When you give written notice that the employment will end, you must specify the notice period and the final date of employment.

As redundancy can mean that there is no longer any work for the individual to do, you may prefer them not to attend work during the notice period. I am often asked if employers can end the employment immediately and make a payment instead of notice. This is called a payment in lieu of notice (PILON). There are difficulties with doing this. If it was not envisaged in the past, there may not be a provision in the terms and conditions of employment allowing you to make a PILON. You can still offer to make a PILON instead of the individual working their notice but they do not have to accept it.[45] In reality, most people do accept it but you cannot require them to unless there is a clause in the terms and conditions of employment.

An alternative to PILON is to offer an employee 'garden leave' during their notice period. Garden leave (sometimes known as gardening leave) means that, while their employment continues until the end of their notice period, the employee does not have to work.[46] They are still paid and receive benefits as normal and they are still bound by their contract of employment. The benefit for you as the employer is that they cannot work elsewhere during this time and they have to remain available for work if you need them. Garden leave is only a safe option if there is a clause in the terms and conditions of employment allowing it. If there is no such clause, trying to force the employee to take garden leave can be considered a breach of their contract and they can claim constructive dismissal. It may be that the safest option is to allow the employee to continue to work during their notice period.

They are entitled to take time off during their notice period to find another job (attend interviews, meet with employment agencies, etc). There are rules about how much time off they are entitled to but, in practice, it is often best to allow them whatever time they need. Even if they are working their notice, they are unlikely to be productive during that time. As with everything during the redundancy process, the best option is to talk to the employee about what works best for them and you.

Skills and knowledge handover

Another issue you need to think about during the employee's notice period is the handover of their knowledge and skills to others who remain in employment. This may seem to contradict previous advice about the reasons for redundancy but, while you might not need particular skills or knowledge in the future (hence the redundancy), you may still need them in the short term. If it is only a small part of someone's role, it may not be possible to keep them on to do that particular job, but they may be reluctant to pass on their knowledge.

This can be contentious. From the redundant employee's perspective, you are making them redundant because they don't have the right skills and knowledge and yet you expect them to do a handover to other people. It needs to be carefully handled as they may have crucial and exclusive knowledge about how part of the business works. This is a good example of the importance of having documented processes and practices within individual roles, particularly if only one person has the knowledge.

It may be that you need a redundant employee to stay on longer than expected to complete a specific piece of work or a customer contract. Again, this is likely to be contentious and you may need to consider offering some kind of retention bonus or motivational payment to persuade them to stay long enough to complete the work but to leave due to redundancy after that.

Do you need a settlement agreement?

A settlement agreement is a document in which an employee agrees to waive their rights to make legal claims against the employer.[47] Employers often feel that they need to use settlement agreements as part of the redundancy process to protect their business from unhappy employees bringing any legal action.

In my view, if a redundancy process is carried out properly, fairly and with compassion and kindness, it is not necessary to use a settlement agreement. If you do use them, it can be costly and it doesn't always provide the protection you seek.

Settlement agreements need to include a payment to compensate the individual for waiving their legal rights in addition to their notice pay and redundancy pay. The sum needs to be big enough to persuade the employee that it is worth agreeing to. The employee has the right to get independent legal advice on the settlement agreement and whether or not it is fair, and the employer is also responsible for paying a sum towards their legal costs.

Help to offer

If you are looking at redundancies in your workplace, you are likely trying to cut costs. You may worry that any help you could provide would be costly and difficult to justify but providing help and support to someone who is facing the loss of their job and income need not cost much or anything at all. Losing your job is tough and any help which an employer can offer will be welcomed and appreciated.

Large corporate organisations may offer outplacement services – often provided by a third party – that can be costly, especially for a large number of redundancies.[48] For a smaller employer with a limited budget, this may still be a financially viable option, or there are other ways of providing similar support such as interview practice, help with CV writing and job applications or career coaching.

Other ways to help those in your business who are facing redundancies include:

- Providing accurate and timely information, especially financial information.

- Making sure redundancy payments and associated payments (notice pay, final salary, outstanding holiday pay) are accurate and paid speedily.

- Communicating clearly and allowing people to ask questions (even the same ones over again).

- Providing confidential counselling if needed (this may, and arguably should, be a benefit you offer in any event).

- Offering financial advice and counselling (again, this may be a benefit you offer already to all staff).

- Supplying accurate and helpful references (not just 'worked here from x to y date in z job').

- Ensuring they are properly considered for vacancies in your business or any connected company (if you are a small business, you could consider liaising with other local employers to see if there are opportunities).

- Keeping the door open for future opportunities.

- Providing local job vacancies lists.

- Setting up (for larger redundancy programmes or site closures) a 'jobs fair'.

- Giving access to recruitment agencies.

- Allowing time off for job hunting.

- Asking them what help they need and giving it where possible (or explaining clearly, carefully and kindly why it is not possible).

- Checking on their mental health and giving them advice on where to get help if they are struggling. Reassuring them that it's OK to not be OK.

- Providing some training and re-skilling so wider options are open to them.

- Giving advice about self-employment.

This list is not exhaustive and you may think of other ways to help and support your redundant employees. They will also have other suggestions when you talk to them.

MAKE THE DIFFERENCE

I can still remember the first time I had to tell someone their job was redundant. Even though it was over twenty-five years ago, I remember the man's face and how difficult it was to tell him that he wouldn't have a job with the company anymore.

It was the hardest thing I had ever done in my working life and I didn't get much sleep the night before. Even back then it was a regular part of the job in HR but that doesn't make it any easier.

The employee was able to take early retirement and I remember spending a great deal of time following up on details about small pension pots and insurance policies. He had worked for the business for over thirty years and had forgotten many of these different pots of money. Finding them all made a difference. In financial terms, it gave him and his family a little more during his retirement, but it made a huge difference to the pain he felt going through redundancy and his feelings about the company.

He was incredibly grateful – I still have the thank you card he sent me. He left our employment with the firm belief that he had been treated well and fairly and he told other people that. Even though we had to make people redundant, the company's reputation was enhanced.

Summary

In this chapter, we have looked at the start of the dismissal process. We discussed the notice period and the different alternatives to having unproductive employees working up to their final day of employment. We also looked at ways in which you can help your employee find another job or move on to the next phase of their working life. In the next chapter, we will discuss the financial implications of redundancy for the employee.

9
Implement: Money

The employee's feelings about the redundancy and the employer will greatly rest on the financial consequences. There is a common misconception that redundancy pay is a large amount that can set someone up for life. For a fortunate few, this might be true. In the vast majority of cases, the redundancy compensation is smaller than anticipated. When it comes to supporting your family and living on redundancy pay while you seek another job, it can run out quickly. In this chapter, we consider redundancy pay and the other financial aspects of redundancy and explore how they can smooth – or worsen – the redundancy process.

Redundancy pay

There is a statutory minimum redundancy payment if an employee has worked for you for two years or longer.[49] The calculation of how much statutory redundancy pay a person is entitled to depends on various factors: their age, their length of employment with you, whether they work regular or variable hours, and the amount they earn per week (capped at a figure published by the government each year). As with many statutory minimums, it is a small amount and does not go far towards compensating someone for losing their job.

Sadly, many businesses will only be in a position to pay the statutory amount. When I am advising businesses about how to improve their reputation, employee engagement and ability to recruit, I encourage them to consider what benefits they might be able to offer in addition to the statutory payment. It is hard for small businesses to compete with large corporate companies in terms of the package they offer employees. Enhanced redundancy pay might be a way that they can improve their offer.

Many larger organisations will offer enhanced redundancy pay – that is, something better than the statutory minimum. A company may enhance redundancy pay by offering a higher amount to people who volunteer for redundancy and are made redundant (not all volunteers are accepted – see Chapter 5). It can entice people to volunteer for redundancy and be useful when a company is willing to accept volunteers.

As part of your planning, you need to agree on one standard calculation method for defining redundancy pay and this needs to comply with the legal requirements.[50] Redundancy rules and calculations can be complex even for HR and finance professionals so providing worked examples to representatives and those affected and the data/formulae on which the payment will be based can be helpful.

Whatever the amount, and the method of arriving at it, the calculation must be done early in the process for each individual at risk. The figures can then be shared with individuals as part of the individual consultation process, subject to confirmation of the final amount once notice is given and the final date of employment is known. Problems and misunderstandings can then be ironed out early – well before the payment is due to be made. Having the financial figures in hand can help the individual's planning process. You also need to tell them when and how you will make the payment. In any event, you must share the figures, including how they have been calculated, with the employee during their notice period.

Check and double-check the amounts. It is amazing how many different ways a typical payroll and/or HR team can calculate redundancy payments and come up with slightly different figures. It can be stressful if the employee is given incorrect figures or paid an incorrect amount. I have seen both and it is upsetting for the individual and embarrassing for the employer. The redundancy pay should be paid to the employee no later than their final payday.[51] Make sure it is paid when and how you told the employee it would be. Late payment is also stressful and unkind.

Enhanced terms

I mentioned earlier in this chapter that companies must offer the statutory redundancy payment terms as a minimum but they can choose to enhance what they offer. The most common enhancement is for a company to calculate redundancy pay based on the employee's actual weekly payment rather than the capped statutory weekly payment amount. This can make a redundancy payment much more generous, particularly for higher-paid employees.

Another common enhancement is to offer double the statutory redundancy payment. You can also make employees eligible to receive a redundancy payment from the first day of employment rather than requiring them to have been employed for at least two years. You could increase the number of weeks paid for each year of service.

These are all ways of enhancing the redundancy payment. You can offer any that you wish, either as a contractual entitlement (ie by including the enhanced pay in the terms and conditions of employment and the company's redundancy policy) or as a one-off for a specific redundancy exercise. Although, if it is a one-off, it can set a precedent for future redundancy processes and you may find you need to stick to it in future to avoid any potential discrimination or unfair treatment. It is more likely that a company will offer enhanced redundancy terms as a contractual benefit.

If you provide enhanced terms, it can be helpful to show clearly how generous the employer has been by providing both the statutory minimum figure and the employer enhancement.

Of course, many businesses just pay the statutory amount and there is nothing wrong with that. After all, redundancy is often due to financial challenges and it is useful for a company to be able to keep the costs as low as possible – they have a habit of growing hugely, without any additional impetus.

Whatever the size of your business, it is crucial that you understand that these variations are possible. Many businesses transfer employees from another business entity – a Transfer of Undertakings (Protection of Employment) or TUPE transfer (which we touched on in Chapter 1).[52] This is when a business, or part of a business, is transferred from one employer to another. The TUPE regulations are legislation put in place to protect an employee who is moved from their employer to another employer to do largely the same job. This can happen with small employers, and it might affect only one employee, or it can be a large employer, affecting many employees. The legislation is there to protect the employees – it requires that an employee's terms and conditions of employment must remain as good as they were with the original employer. If you have acquired an employee through a transfer from another employer, you might find that their terms and conditions of employment are different from your standard terms, including the terms of any redundancy payment. If the previous employer had enhanced redundancy terms, your transferred employee still has the right to those and may be entitled to a higher redundancy payment.

This is why it is so important during the planning process to consider the terms of employment of each employee who is put at risk of redundancy so that you can calculate the potential costs to the business. A word of warning – it is not fair or lawful to select one employee for redundancy over another because their redundancy payment will be lower.

Early retirement

Employers have asked me if they can offer their employees early retirement instead of redundancy. The truth is that an employee whose job is redundant is entitled to redundancy (and redundancy pay if they are eligible). Employees who are nearing pensionable age may decide to take advantage of any early retirement option that is offered by their pension scheme but that does not preclude their entitlement to a redundancy payment. You may find that some employees are keener to volunteer for redundancy if they can take their pension but it is not a factor you can consider when deciding who is at risk of redundancy.

Long-term sickness

Another factor that can cause employers concern is what to do when they are making an employee's job redundant and the employee is off sick. Sometimes, people go off sick when they find out they are being placed at risk of redundancy. Often, they go off with stress or anxiety due to the situation. Their sickness can make it difficult for the employer to proceed. There may be cases when you doubt the genuine nature of the sickness and worry the employee is trying to use it as a way to escape redundancy.

It is difficult to provide general advice on this situation as much depends on the individual case. As with any sickness, I recommend that employers assume the sickness is genuine and treat the individual the same way as any other employee. It may be necessary to get a medical report to assess whether or not an individual is so sick that they cannot attend a consultation meeting. If the absence is caused by stress, a doctor may feel it is beneficial for the individual to attend the meeting to relieve the source of stress but, if the medical report says a meeting is not possible, you are unable to go ahead until the employee's health improves. If the absence is due to an ailment such as a broken leg, it may be possible to hold the consultation in a different venue (such as the employee's home) or over a video link.

If a whole team is facing redundancy, the person who is off sick cannot be left out, even if they are absent. In this case, you need to make every attempt to consult with them, even if it is delayed while they are given time to recover. You might be able to consult via video (Zoom, Microsoft Teams, etc), in writing or through a third party. The crucial thing is to be fair and make every attempt to consult.

If someone is off sick long term, the redundancy pay will depend on what provision you have in place. Some companies have a long-term sickness/incapacity insurance scheme that will continue to pay an employee who is off sick until they reach normal retirement age. The payment is likely to be at a much lower rate than their salary and will be subject to stringent medical checks, but if there is such a scheme in place and someone is benefitting from it, my advice is to leave it in place instead of redundancy. Most such schemes remove the employee from the headcount anyway and the individual should not be included in the selection pool for redundancy. This is always a tricky situation – organisations should seek professional guidance to see what alternatives there might be and tread carefully.

If someone is off sick long term and there is no such insurance scheme, they may still be in your headcount. It will depend on your sickness absence policy, which may allow you to terminate the employment of an employee who is unlikely to recover or be able to return to work within a reasonable timeframe. If that is the case, you may be able to manage the situation through that policy. If there is no such option, you may need to make the individual redundant and make a redundancy payment. There is a risk that the employee could claim unfair selection for redundancy but it may be a risk you feel is worth taking. In such a situation, I suggest that you take professional HR advice.

Summary

In this chapter, we have considered the payments that must be made to people who are facing redundancy. We have looked at additional amounts you might choose to pay and why they are a good idea. We have also considered some of the areas that can be difficult for employers when they are paying redundant employees.

PART FIVE
THE AFTERMATH

In this final part, we look at what happens after the redundancy has taken place, both for the (ex-) employee and the company. This can be an important factor in whether your company survives and thrives and should not be overlooked.

10

Review: Beyond Redundancy

Your redundant employee has reached their final date and left your employment. You have made their redundancy payment and they have moved on to the next stage of their working life. That doesn't mean you can or should forget about them. In this chapter, we are going to look at what happens after the redundancy, whether there is anything more you can or should do for the employee and why. We also take a look at the people who remain in your employment – the survivors.

After the redundancy

As part of the consultation with employees at risk of redundancy, you should have explored how you can help them to move on from redundancy. If you included this vital step as part of your consultation process, you will do much to foster a healthy relationship with departing employees. This has several benefits. Firstly, your reputation as an employer is less likely to suffer and may even be enhanced. This can lead to easier recruitment and better customer relationships. Secondly, your ex-employees may be willing to return to work for you again in the future, helping you to get more out of the investment you made in training and developing them. Thirdly, it will improve the relationship and trust you have with your remaining workforce who watched the redundancy from the sidelines.

We have already explored the help you can offer in earlier chapters but it is worth revisiting briefly since many of these supports continue after the employee has left your employment. Some examples are:

1. Financial advice, maybe via an independent financial advisor.

2. Counselling to help them adjust to the situation or for other reasons.

3. Outplacement services to help them get another job.

4. CV writing and references.

5. Flagging up other opportunities and/or provide guidance on where to get advice on how to make a living, set up their own business, foster, make a career change or volunteer.

6. Paying for training courses.

Keeping in touch

Have you thought about the advantages of keeping in touch with employees after they have been made redundant? You may think this would be time wasted – why would you bother keeping in touch with employees who have stopped working for you, especially if they left under difficult circumstances or it was an awkward parting?

This is where having handled their redundancy fairly and with kindness and compassion starts to pay dividends. The parting may have been awkward, but if you handled the redundancy process well, they will still think you were a good employer. They may be open to working for you again and recommend you to people as a supplier or an employer.

I recommend keeping in touch with all your ex-employees where practicable. This may only mean staying connected on social media or keeping them on a newsletter mailing list. It doesn't have to be a continuing relationship – it can be keeping the lines of communication open.

If you treat people well when they work for you and they are happy in your employment, they will remember their employment and your company with warm feelings and be more inclined to say good things about you to other people. This can enhance your reputation, or at least prevent damage to your good name. In a tight labour market, this can be an invaluable tool. As I touched on earlier, social media is a fact of modern life and any employer ignores it at their peril. You want to avoid negative posts on social media from disgruntled employees. A large proportion of job-seekers look on sites like Glassdoor to find out about prospective employers and you do not want negative reports online about your company.

When the time comes to increase your headcount again, wouldn't it be good to be able to re-employ an ex-employee in whom you invested and who already knows your business? Having the option of messaging a former employee via social media to find out if they would be interested in returning to your employment could save you expensive recruitment costs.

Re-employing

I sometimes run free Q&A sessions on redundancy and I have noticed a pattern of questions about re-employing people once you have made them redundant.

The questions I have seen are along the following lines:

- Can I re-employ someone I made redundant?

- Do I need to leave a gap before I offer someone whom I made redundant another job?

- Can I use someone as a consultant if I made them redundant?

In my experience, employee representatives often ask that those made redundant are first on the list to be recruited when an upswing happens. I want to address this subject as it is important.

Many HR professionals, and even lawyers, will advise you to leave a gap of at least six months before you re-employ someone but that is not strictly true. The legal position is that a redundancy must be genuine and you must be able to evidence the genuineness if you face a legal challenge. You need to be able to show that there was no prospect of being able to retain those employees. It is possible, although extremely unlikely, that the situation could change the day after your redundant employees left your business. A new, unexpected order could come in, for example. If you could evidence that it was large enough to enable you to employ those people again, you could consider re-employing employees who have just left. It is risky and certain downsides mean that, in general terms, you are best to wait a period of at least six months before considering re-employment.

If you want to re-employ someone soon after their redundancy, it begs the question why did you make them redundant in the first place? Unless there is clear and strong evidence that your business situation has changed dramatically, the redundancy could be considered unfair dismissal and you would find it difficult to defend your position.

Another major downside is that you have already paid their redundancy payment and you would not be able to claim that back. A further disadvantage is that the redundancy may have damaged your relationship with the employee and the trust between you. You may find that they are not the same loyal, willing employee as before. They will be wary of being made redundant again as soon as it suits you.

I have often seen people being re-employed almost immediately but on a consultancy basis. The same risks apply so I would avoid this, especially as it can be an expensive way of employing someone. Additionally, an ex-employee working on a consultancy basis is likely to be upsetting to your other employees.

If you are thinking about re-employing a redundant employee, you should take professional advice before you go ahead.

The survivors

What about the people left in the workplace after a redundancy programme – the 'survivors'?

Initially, they are likely to feel a sense of relief – they still have paid employment – but the feelings that follow may cause them sleepless nights or worse. They may fear that the axe will fall again and they will be selected next time. If the business is in such dire straits that it needs to make redundancies, will it be able to turn around and become successful again? There is great pressure on them to perform well – even if it is self-imposed. They might feel anxiety about the potential reorganisation to address gaps left by those who have been made redundant. People often struggle with change, particularly if it has been 'forced' upon them. Will there be extra work for them, now there are fewer people to do it? They might miss the colleagues who have moved on, especially if they worked closely together.

There will be myriad other feelings and reactions and, as a manager, you won't know what they are unless you talk to the survivors and find out. At this time, more than any other, they need a friendly ear, support, understanding and reassurance. How you look after the survivors may well make the difference between the business merely surviving and actively thriving in the future.

Fear for own position

I have often seen that once the redundancy process is over, the people left behind are fearful about their own position within the company. They no longer feel safe and secure in their employment. This is a dangerous time for employers. It is the time when people start to look around for a more secure job. They might be open to being poached by your competitors.

The news of your redundancy programme will be out in the world. Other employers may have been keeping tabs on your redundant employees. This can work in your favour as they might offer jobs to the people you let go but, if that has been unsuccessful or they have more vacancies than candidates, you might find that they try to tempt your remaining employees away. Your redundant employees may give new employers the names of former colleagues who fit the description for vacancies, especially if they were friends with your remaining employees. You may experience some churn in your business and some of your employees want to move on.

How can an employer prevent too many resignations following a redundancy programme? As always, listening to your employees is a good place to start. An employee opinion survey can be a useful way of testing your remaining employees' morale. Listen to their fears, concerns, dreams, goals and desires. You will have a vision of where you want your business to be, your goals and objectives. Hopefully, this vision played a big part in your planning before the redundancy took place. Now is the time to start sharing that vision with your remaining employees, giving them an insight into what their future with your organisation might look like and the opportunities available to them.

This is the time to improve your workforce communications, to build and improve your methods of engaging with your employees. It is the time for monitoring absence and the reasons for it, rewarding innovations by employees and celebrating their successes. It may also be sensible to consider whether to offer a long-term retention bonus to critical employees.

Grieving process

It is important to think about how your employees might be feeling. If working relationships were close and productive, there may be a sense almost of bereavement. Employees will be grieving the loss of their colleagues. This will be exacerbated by their fear of losing their own positions and the potential increased workload.

If the redundancy was a means to reduce costs for the business, it may be that the workload has not decreased as much as anticipated. If an employer simply expects the survivors to take on work that used to be done by redundant colleagues, it can feel like an insult, particularly if people were already feeling stretched. It might be worth thinking about improving your processes, looking into digital or automated initiatives and considering more flexibility in roles and location to mitigate the effects.

The emotional impact of missing a friend or colleague is doubled by the impact of more work. It can be a step too far and you may find an increased rate of sickness absence. Monitoring absence and the reasons for it becomes even more important to understand the pressures those employees are facing. Like an elastic band, emotional resilience can only stretch so far – when it becomes too stretched, it will break.

Part of your redundancy planning might have included increasing (or implementing) mental health first-aid support. Many companies provide access to counsellors as an employment benefit. At this time, this benefit might be used far more. If you don't have the resources to offer access to counsellors, the least you can do is provide advice and guidance on external help that might be available to people. Many external bodies (mental health charities, for example) can offer support in the form of information leaflets or helplines.

Managers are employees too and much of the workload and stress involved in a redundancy programme falls on them. Your managers may be grieving too.

If they managed a tight-knit and effective team, and have to re-group and manage a smaller set of people with a similar workload, they are going to feel the gaps. It is important for an employer not to overlook managers and the help and support they might need. It might be as simple as a forum where they can talk to other managers in the same position or it might be something more in-depth. They need the same support, encouragement, view of future opportunities and friendly ear as your other remaining employees.

Summary

In this chapter, we have considered what can happen after redundancy. We have looked at the help we can offer ex-employees. We have looked at the potential advantages of keeping in touch with ex-employees and the possibility of re-employing them after they have been made redundant. We have thought about what support the people left behind to carry the business forward might need and we have looked at methods and initiatives to help the business to survive and thrive in its next phase.

11
Review: The Full Circle

We have completed the redundancy programme and the employees have left. Our survivors are settling into the new regime. What is there still to cover? Redundancy doesn't always go smoothly or according to plan and, in this final chapter, we look at things that can go wrong and how to avoid or manage them. It is also a good opportunity to look at how we can learn lessons from the redundancy process and make sure they are included in the next redundancy programme which (of course) we hope will never be needed.

What can go wrong?

Even the best-laid plans can go wrong. Redundancy often doesn't run according to plan and there are pitfalls and potholes along the way. We are dealing with people, and people are all different. No matter how fair your process seems, how careful your planning or how wide-ranging the support you offer, there is nearly always someone – an employee or a manager or a survivor – who doesn't conform to the pattern and can derail the process.

Some people are simply difficult to deal with. If they are stressed, frightened, think they know more than you do, have a friend who is a lawyer or a relative who has been through this before, or any number of other factors, they can make the process difficult and stressful for everyone concerned. Sometimes that is their aim. They are unhappy about what is happening to them and they want the business or their manager to suffer. More often, there is a communication breakdown or a misunderstanding. You need to be prepared for the unexpected and flexible enough to take a detour from the planned path.

You might get your first inkling that there are choppy waters ahead during the consultation. An employee might come into consultation with all guns blazing, ready to take you on and prove to you that you have got it wrong and they should not be made redundant. Most of the time, a willingness to listen to them, patience and careful explanations can change the course of the conversation. Other employees may not show how they are feeling or say much. That doesn't mean they have come to terms with the situation or that they are dealing with it well.

It is not uncommon for someone to go off sick during the consultation period. You may be concerned that they are not really sick and are just trying to delay the process. This is rarely the case and the sickness is often genuine. Stress can do funny things to people. We have talked about sickness in previous chapters and my advice is to treat all sickness as genuine and manage it through your sickness rules. The person will eventually become well enough to return to work (in which case you can continue the redundancy process) or they will be considered unfit to work again – in which case you can deal with it through the sickness absence route, which can lead to dismissal.

People can use all sorts of delaying tactics to prevent you from getting to the point of confirming their redundancy. They might find it difficult to identify someone to accompany them to consultation meetings. You don't have to keep accepting their delay. They need to find another companion or attend unaccompanied if that is the issue. I have seen cases where people fail to turn up to consultation meetings in the mistaken belief that if you don't consult with them the redundancy cannot go ahead. That is true up to a point, but if you can show that you have rearranged meetings and worked around issues to enable them to attend and they keep failing to do so, eventually you may need to carry out the process in writing rather than face to face. As long as you have been reasonable and accommodated their needs as far as possible, you won't go far wrong.

Another delaying tactic is to produce a grievance about something during the redundancy consultation. There is a common belief that redundancy has to be put on hold while a grievance is investigated and managed but this is not the case. If the grievance is about the redundancy or any aspect of the redundancy, it is perfectly acceptable to deal with it as part of the redundancy process or even as part of an appeal. If the grievance is unrelated to the redundancy, it can be investigated and heard separately from the consultation during the same timeframe. You must manage the grievance and give an outcome before terminating the employment but you do not have to delay the consultation. You can still confirm the redundancy and give notice after the outcome of the grievance.

Other pitfalls

We have talked about the importance of getting communications right throughout the redundancy programme. One of the major pitfalls in any redundancy process is inconsistent communications. This is why a communications plan is a vital part of redundancy planning. It is critical that your managers (and other stakeholders) are involved in producing the communications plan and understand the importance of sticking to it. If mixed messages are given or if people miss a critical part of the communications, it can cause disruption, resentment and anger.

The same is true when inappropriate promises are made to employees or they are given an incorrect impression about what is – and is not – possible or available. This often stems from poor communication because a manager is trying to be kind or soften the blow when, in reality, they are giving a mixed or incorrect message and adding confusion and distrust into an already difficult mix.

Another thing that can go wrong is a rushed consultation. Understandably, a manager (particularly one with little experience of redundancy) might want to rush through the consultation to 'get it over with' but that is not helpful for the employee on the receiving end of the message. By the same token, managers can sometimes be guilty of paying lip service to the process and not engaging with the employee or the consultation. Employees can sense when a manager is rushing the process and not fully committed to supporting them through a difficult time. This causes further resentment and a feeling of being undervalued. These dangers can be mitigated by having a checklist (see Chapter 7) or script for the consultation process. As discussed in Chapter 4, a script can give an inexperienced manager confidence and a sense of control, and I know managers who have found it useful. The inherent danger in this approach is that if the manager simply reads from the script or ticks off the checklist, it can increase the employee's frustration and cynicism. If you want to provide a script or a checklist, you need to also provide training and support for your managers so they can use it as a prompt rather than reading from it and giving the impression of ignorance or being uninterested.

Review and revise

Once the redundancy process is over, it is time to consider the lessons you have learnt from the process which might be useful for future reference if you ever face another redundancy situation.

Here are important questions to ask yourself about your redundancy programme:

- What support did you give those you made redundant to find other work? What was the take-up of that support? Did people find it useful or would they have preferred something else? What is the cost-versus-benefit analysis of that support?

- How meaningful was the consultation? Were you open to suggestions about how redundancy might be avoided? Were there any useful suggestions?

Was there anything that might be worth investigating for future reference?

- How fair was your selection process? Did it identify the people you would have expected to be put at risk? Were there any complaints? What were they and were they valid?

- Have you kept the door open for a future employment relationship or have you burnt your bridges? Would you be interested in re-employing any of your redundant employees at a later date?

- What support have you been able to offer to those who 'survived' redundancy and remain employed by you? Have you temperature-tested how well the workforce has settled post-redundancy? Have you received any resignations? Has productivity risen to or beyond pre-redundancy levels? What do your attendance records look like?

- What steps are you putting in place to avoid future redundancy? Could you have prevented the redundancy through some prior planning? Did anything new come out in consultation that might have had a bearing on why you were in a redundancy situation?

- Did you use the redundancy process to 'get rid of deadwood'? If so, it raises questions about your management style and you may want to consider whether you would benefit from management training or rethinking your approach.

- How fair and kind was your whole redundancy process? If you, your partner or your children had been made redundant by your company, would you feel you or they were treated fairly and kindly? Are redundant employees happy to keep in touch with the company? Have there been any appeals and tribunal claims?

Considering these questions – and the truthful answers to them – might reveal useful insights into how to approach a redundancy programme in the future.

Update policy

Having reviewed the process and lessons learnt from your redundancy programme, this is a good time to review – and update – your redundancy policy. You will now have a good idea about how the policy worked and whether it is a true reflection of your approach and the way things pan out in real life. Policies are necessary for a variety of reasons but they are not useful until they have been tested in a real situation. It is all very well to have aspirations for how to manage a given process but those aspirations might not be achievable or realistic. I help businesses to write and produce policies for a wide variety of situations and they do not come to life unless they have been put into practice.

This review at the end of your redundancy programme is incredibly useful to keep your policies and processes up-to-date and practical. It may seem like extra work but now is the ideal time to make this assessment. It can make a huge difference if you have to manage a redundancy situation again. Chapter 3 looked at planning and this final review and revision is a big part of that planning for similar situations in the future.

Summary

This final chapter has looked at what can go wrong with your redundancy programme. You have considered the lessons you can take from the whole process and how to action those updates through updating your policy to help with planning any future redundancy programmes you might face. This completes the circle.

Conclusion

Here we are at the end. Having read the book, you will have an excellent foundation in how to manage a redundancy situation fairly and kindly, which will help your employees – those facing redundancy and those who remain – and your managers.

We started by considering the reasons why your business is facing redundancy and whether it is the right way forward. We looked at your goals and plans for the future and where you want your business to be. We also considered the costs of redundancy and whether making redundancies will achieve the cost reduction you require. Redundancy is hugely time-consuming, costly and stressful for everyone involved and we asked whether it is worth it. Then we looked at possible alternatives to redundancy and whether there might be a better way to achieve your aims.

If redundancy is unavoidable for your business, we considered how best to plan for redundancy including your redundancy policy; a specific plan for your redundancy programme; what needs to be in such a plan; how many roles must go and which types of roles; what help you might want to offer to your redundant employees. We looked at the support and training you should give your managers to enable them to handle the selection of and consultation with employees. We also had a brief look at the most important legalities of redundancy.

We spent time considering how to select people to face redundancy with compassion and kindness in a way that works for your business plans. We looked at collective consultation with trade unions and employee representatives and why it is critical to the success of the redundancy programme. We had a more in-depth look at consulting with individual employees who are at risk of redundancy, why it is important to get it right and the benefits to both the employees and the business. We also thought about the reactions you might see from employees when you give the message.

Having selected people for redundancy and consulted with them about it, we looked at the redundancy dismissal process and how to support your employees through it. We considered the financial aspects of redundancy for the affected employees and what financial support you need or might want to give.

Once people have left the business through redundancy, we looked at maintaining an ongoing relationship with them, how you can continue to support them and the benefits for your business. There might even be a time when you would look at re-employing them. We talked about how best to support your remaining employees – the survivors.

Finally, we looked at things that can go wrong during the process. We considered what we had learnt through the process and how to use that to plan for another time.

You now know how to manage redundancy, with love.

Throughout the book, I have pointed out pitfalls and areas in which you might need professional support to manage your redundancy process to make sure that it is fair, kind and compassionate and works for your business and future goals. For more information about the services I provide or if you want to pick my brains, please visit my website: www.heartfelthr.com

If you want help getting started, you can download a template redundancy policy using this link: www. heartfelthr.com/book-offer. You will be asked for your name and email address and will be added to my mailing list. You will need to enter the following password to access the download: HHRRWL01

Glossary

Acas The Advisory, Conciliation and Arbitration Service

Agency staff/Agency temps Staff employed by an agency hired out to a third-party employer

Appeal process An internal process to allow an employee to appeal against a sanction/dismissal imposed by their employer

Apprentices People who are employed or provided through a training organisation to learn their trade on-the-job

Capped payments or capped salaries Payments or salaries that have a set maximum

Collective consultation An employer's consultation with employee representatives or trade union representatives about proposed dismissals

Contractor A self-employed worker who is hired by an employer to do specific work in a specific timeframe

Direct discrimination When someone is treated differently and worse than someone else because of who they are or whom people think they are

Disability A condition of the body or mind which makes it more difficult for someone to do certain things or interact with others

Dismissal When the employer ends the employment

Early retirement Retirement before the 'normal retirement age' expected by a pension provider

Employee representatives People elected by their colleagues or appointed to represent employees

Employment tribunal An independent tribunal that makes decisions in employment disputes about employment law

Enhanced redundancy pay When those made redundant receive a higher rate of redundancy pay than the statutory minimum

Entitlement to be accompanied The right for an employee to bring an agreed companion to support them in an employment situation

External redundancy consultant An advisor about redundancy who does not work for the employer

False redundancy A dismissal said to be for redundancy which hides the true reason for the dismissal (ie not a genuine redundancy)

Fixed-term contract An employment contract that is for a set time and has a defined end date

Furlough When a company could not operate or did not have enough work to employ people during the coronavirus pandemic, they could put people on leave (furlough) and the government paid a percentage of their salary so the employer could retain their services

Garden leave or gardening leave When an employee is told to remain away from work during their notice period but remains available for work and on normal pay

Indirect discrimination Where a practice or policy applies to everyone in the same way but has a worse effect on some people

Individual consultation An individual meeting with an employee who is facing redundancy to explain and discuss the reasons for and effects of that redundancy

Interns People (normally but not always students) who work for an employer (either paid or unpaid) to gain work experience or for a qualification

Notice period The amount of time an employee must work for an employer after they have resigned or been dismissed

Outplacement A service to help employees who are leaving a company to plan their next employment or training, etc

Payment in lieu of notice (PILON) A payment made to an employee who is leaving where they do not have to work their notice period, but are paid an equivalent amount instead

Recruitment freeze A period when a company does not hire anyone, take on any maternity cover or replace anybody who is leaving

Redeployment Where an employee moves from one job to another one within the same company or a sister company

Redundancy Dismissal when an employer needs to reduce their workforce (see Chapter 1 for the legal definition)

Restructure A process that aims to make the business more efficient (often includes redundancy or changes to jobs and teams)

Retention bonus An additional payment made to encourage an employee to remain in their job for a longer period or to thank them for so doing (often paid after a set period)

Sabbatical A paid period of leave to allow an employee to travel or study while their job remains open to them

Secondment A temporary work placement to a different area from the one where an employee normally works

Selection The process of choosing which employees will be put at risk of being made redundant

Selection criteria The measures used to choose which employees will be made redundant

Selection pool A group of people doing the same or similar work where one, some or all people in the pool will face redundancy

Selection scoring A system to allot points against the selection criteria for each person in a selection pool

Settlement agreement A legally binding agreement between the employer and the employee under which the employee agrees not to pursue legal claims in exchange for a severance payment

Statutory redundancy pay The minimum payment set out by the government that an employer must pay an employee when they are made redundant

Suitable alternative An alternative job within the company that prevents a redundancy – it should be 'suitable' in terms of skills, pay, terms and hours

Survivors The people who remain working for a company after a redundancy programme

TUPE Transfer of Undertakings (Protection of Employment) – legal protection for an employee that applies when an employee's role and the employee move to another employer

Unfair dismissal Where the reason given for dismissal was not the real one or was unfair or the employer acted unreasonably

Voluntary redundancy Where an employee puts themselves forward for a redundancy before being selected

Work placements A period of supervised work (for a schoolchild or student), which is a chance to experience working in a specific role in a company

References

1 The Advisory, Conciliation and Arbitration Service or Acas is a government-funded, independent public body that provides free and impartial advice to employers, employees and their representatives (acas.org.uk)

2 Redundancy is not the correct way to dismiss a difficult employee. If you want more guidance on this subject, take professional HR advice

3 Employment Rights Act 1996, Pt XI, c 2, s 139, www.legislation.gov.uk/ukpga/1996/18/section/139

4 The Transfer of Undertakings (Protection of Employment) Regulations 2006, No 246, www.legislation.gov.uk/uksi/2006/246/introduction/made

5 'Redundancy pay', UK Government (no date), www.gov.uk/staff-redundant/redundancy-pay, accessed 7 September 2022

6 'When an employee is not required to work their notice', Acas (17 May 2021), www.acas.org.uk/notice-periods/when-an-employee-is-not-required-to-work-their-notice, accessed 7 September 2022

7 'Taking holiday before leaving a job', UK Government (no date), www.gov.uk/holiday-entitlement-rights/taking-holiday-before-leaving-a-job, accessed 7 September 2022

8 'Suitable alternative employment', UK Government (no date), www.gov.uk/redundancy-your-rights/suitable-alternative-employment, accessed 7 September 2022

9 'How to hold collective consultation', Acas (23 July 2021), www.acas.org.uk/collective-consultation-redundancy/how-to-hold-collective-consultation, accessed 7 September 2022

10 'Redundancy Q&As', Chartered Institute of Personnel and Development – CIPD (6 April 2022), www.cipd.co.uk/knowledge/fundamentals/emp-law/redundancy/questions#gref, accessed 7 September 2022

11 'Lay-offs and short-time working', UK Government (no date), www.gov.uk/staff-redundant/layoffs-and-shorttime-working, accessed 7 September 2022

12 'Lay-offs and short-time working', UK Government (no date), www.gov.uk/staff-redundant/layoffs-and-shorttime-working, accessed 7 September 2022

13 J Owen, 'Capping salaries at £100,000 could save one million jobs, report finds', *People Management* (9 October 2020), www.peoplemanagement.co.uk/article/1742910/capping-salaries-100000-would-save-one-million-jobs-report-finds, accessed 7 September 2022

14 'Redundancy', Acas (no date), www.acas.org.uk/redundancy, ACCESSED 7 SEPTEMBER 2022

15 'Collective consultation for redundancy', Acas (23 July 2021), www.acas.org.uk/collective-consultation-redundancy, accessed 7 September 2022

16 S Evans, 'The dos and don'ts of creating an employee handbook', *People Management* (4 October 2018), www.peoplemanagement.co.uk/article/1745510/dos-donts-creating-employee-handbook, accessed 7 September 2022

17 'Redundancy', Acas (no date), www.acas.org.uk/redundancy, accessed 7 September 2022

18 'Managing staff redundancies: step by step – Step 2: Follow the right process', Acas (6 April 2022), www.acas.org.uk/manage-staff-redundancies/follow-the-right-process, accessed 7 September 2022

19 'Unfair dismissals', UK Government (no date), www.gov.uk/dismiss-staff/unfair-dismissals, accessed 7 September 2022

20 Equality Act 2010, Contents, www.legislation.gov.uk/ukpga/2010/15/contents

21 Employment Rights Act 1996, Pt X, c 1, www.legislation. gov.uk/ukpga/1996/18/part/X/chapter/I

22 Employment Rights Act 1996, Pt X, c 1, s 104, www. legislation.gov.uk/ukpga/1996/18/section/104

23 'Managing staff redundancies: step by step – Step 2: Follow the right process', Acas (6 April 2022), www.acas.org.uk/ manage-staff-redundancies/follow-the-right-process, accessed 7 September 2022

24 Equality Act 2010, Pt II, c 1, s 4, www.legislation.gov.uk/ ukpga/2010/15/section/4

25 'Suitable alternative employment, UK Government (no date), www.gov.uk/redundancy-your-rights/suitable-alternative-employment, accessed 7 September 2022

26 Trade Union and Labour Relations (Consolidation) Act 1992, Pt IV, c 2, s 188, www.legislation.gov.uk/ ukpga/1992/52/section/188

27 'Redundancy consultation, UK Government (no date), www.gov.uk/staff-redundant/redundancy-consultations, accessed 7 September 2022

28 'How your employer must consult you', Acas (6 April 2022), www.acas.org.uk/your-rights-during-redundancy/ how-your-employer-must-consult-you, accessed 7 September 2022

29 'Consultation', UK Government (no date), www.gov. uk/redundancy-your-rights/consultation, accessed 7 September 2022

30 'Form HR1 Advance notification of redundancies: guidance for employers', The Insolvency Service (3 May 2022), www.gov.uk/government/publications/redundancy-payments-form-hr1-advance-notification-of-redundancies/ advanced-notification-of-redundancies-guidance-for-employers#requirement-to-notify-about-potential-redundancies, accessed 7 September 2022

31 'Managing staff redundancies: step by step – Step 5: Select employees for redundancy', Acas (6 April 2022), www.acas. org.uk/manage-staff-redundancies/select-employees-for-redundancy, accessed 7 September 2022

32 *Managing Redundancy for Pregnant Employees or Those on Maternity Leave*, Acas (May 2018), www.acas.org.uk/ sites/default/files/2021-03/managing-redundancy-for-pregnant-employees-or-those-on-maternity-leave.pdf, accessed 7 September 2022

33 Pregnancy and Maternity (Redundancy Protection) Bill, UK Parliament (5 May 2021), https://bills.parliament.uk/bills/2761, accessed 7 September 2022

34 'How common are mental health problems?', Mind (June 2020), www.mind.org.uk/information-support/types-of-mental-health-problems/statistics-and-facts-about-mental-health/how-common-are-mental-health-problems, accessed 7 September 2022

35 'Unfair dismissal', Acas (28 July 2022), www.acas.org.uk/dismissals/unfair-dismissal, accessed 7 September 2022

36 'Disability facts and figures', Scope (no date), www.scope.org.uk/media/disability-facts-figures, accessed 7 September 2022

37 Employment Relations Act 1999, s 10, www.legislation.gov.uk/ukpga/1999/26/section/10

38 'Disciplinary procedure: step by step – Step 4: The disciplinary hearing', Acas (no date), www.acas.org.uk/disciplinary-procedure-step-by-step/step-4-the-disciplinary-hearing, accessed 7 September 2022

39 'Taking another job with your employer', Acas (6 April 2022), www.acas.org.uk/your-rights-during-redundancy/taking-another-job-with-your-employer, accessed 7 September 2022

40 'Taking another job with your employer', Acas (6 April 2022), www.acas.org.uk/your-rights-during-redundancy/taking-another-job-with-your-employer, accessed 7 September 2022

41 *Managing Redundancy for Pregnant Employees or Those on Maternity Leave*, Acas (May 2018), www.acas.org.uk/sites/default/files/2021-03/managing-redundancy-for-pregnant-employees-or-those-on-maternity-leave.pdf, accessed 7 September 2022

42 The Maternity and Parental Leave etc. Regulations 1999, s 10, www.legislation.gov.uk/ukpga/1999/26/section/10

43 'If you feel the redundancy was unfair', Acas (6 April 2022), www.acas.org.uk/your-rights-during-redundancy/appeal-a-redundancy-decision, accessed 7 September 2022

44 'Settlement agreement guidance and templates', Acas (no date), www.acas.org.uk/settlement-agreements, accessed 7 September 2022

45 'Notice periods', Acas (17 May 2021), www.acas.org.uk/notice-periods, accessed 7 September 2022

46 'Gardening leave', UK Government (no date), www.acas.
   org.uk/notice-periods/when-an-employee-is-not-required-
   to-work-their-notice, accessed 7 September 2022
47 Employment Rights Act 1996, Pt XIII, c 2, s 203, www.
   legislation.gov.uk/ukpga/1996/18/section/203
48 'Outplacement', Wikipedia (11 May 2022), https://
   en.wikipedia.org/wiki/Outplacement, accessed 7
   September 2022
49 'Redundancy pay', UK Government (no date), www.gov.
   uk/redundancy-your-rights/redundancy-pay, accessed 7
   September 2022
50 Employment Rights Act 1996, Pt XI, www.legislation.gov.
   uk/ukpga/1996/18/part/XI
51 'How much redundancy pay you get', Acas (6 April 2022),
   www.acas.org.uk/your-rights-during-redundancy/
   redundancy-pay, accessed 7 September 2022
52 'Your TUPE rights – employee advice', Acas (5 August
   2021), www.acas.org.uk/employee-rights-during-a-tupe-
   transfer, accessed 7 September 2022

Acknowledgements

Thank you to my family, friends and colleagues – too numerous to mention – who have supported me while I wrote this book. Special thanks are due to my lovely husband, Julian, who has listened to my ideas, fears and concerns and supported me through them all. Special thanks also to my sister, Judy, who has always believed in me and has been my biggest cheerleader.

I would like to thank my clients for putting their trust in me, for kindly recommending me to others and for letting me tell some of their stories in this book.

Thank you also to my beta readers and praise quote givers: Wendy Martin Green, Gurdip Singh, Alex Hughes, Rupert Brice and Robin Farrar-Hockley.

Their suggestions and comments were invaluable in improving this book.

Thank you to my business networking friends, particularly Fabulous Networking, who have encouraged and supported me throughout this journey. Particular thanks are due to the Fabulous Networking Book Writing Challenge members: Glenda Shawley, Felicity Dwyer, Jacqui McGinn, Nick Keith, Anita Chakraburtty, Sarah Grant, Mandy Dineley Penney, Cathie O'Dea and Graham Le-Gall. They offered suggestions and help when I was flagging and kept me writing when it seemed an impossible task.

Big thanks to Lucy McCarraher for her support and encouragement and thanks to everyone at Rethink Press.

Finally, thank you to my much-loved and sadly missed parents. They showed me that love and compassion are the answer to all problems, especially the difficult and uncomfortable ones.

The Author

Jill's HR career spans nearly thirty years, during which she has worked in and with every type of business, from large globally recognised names to tiny companies with a handful of employees – and many stops in between. As a Chartered Fellow of the Chartered Institute of Personnel and Development (FCIPD), she has advised on complex and difficult redundancy issues.

She has worked in generalist HR roles with an emphasis on employee relations and, in her last employed role, she managed an employee relations team of forty people. She took voluntary redundancy and studied for a postgraduate certificate in Employment Law. After that, she did contract work for some years, dealing mainly with redundancy and TUPE transfers (try explaining UK and European TUPE law to American managers of a global workforce!) with some complex disciplinary and grievance cases thrown in for good measure.

She has run her own HR consultancy business, Heartfelt HR Ltd, for five years specialising in redundancy and disciplinary issues with some policy and contract provision as a bit of light relief. She is a great believer that managing people with kindness and compassion brings great results because happy employees equal a thriving business.

Jill lives at home in rural Oxfordshire with her husband, Julian, and two rescue cats. *Redundancy With Love* is her first book.

Find out more about Jill and connect at:

⊕ www.heartfelthr.com

in www.linkedin.com/in/jill-aburrow